PURE SLIME
50 Incredible Ways To Make Slime Using Household Substances

By Brian Rohrig
Illustrated by Jim Haskins

All experiments in this book are to be performed only under competent adult supervision. Neither the author nor the publisher assume any liability whatsoever for any damage caused or injury sustained while performing the experiments contained in this book.

The brand names of products included in this text are not intended to imply a commercial endorsement of any product.

For Dr. David Keller,
an extraordinary
teacher of teachers

Other Books by Brian Rohrig

150 Captivating Chemistry Experiments Using Household Substances

150 More Captivating Chemistry Experiments Using Household Substances

101 Intriguing Labs, Projects, and Activities for the Chemistry Classroom

39 Amazing Experiments with the Mega-Magnet

39 Fantastic Experiments with the Fizz-Keeper

39 Dazzling Experiments with Dry Ice

Fizz Factor: 50 Amazing Experiments with Soda Pop
(with Steve Spangler)

For ordering information visit
www.fizzbangscience.com

ACKNOWLEDGMENTS

I would like to thank David A. Katz, chemist and educator, for reviewing this manuscript and making many helpful comments and suggestions. David has written and spoken extensively on the practical application of science to everyday life. He has originated several slime recipes and is a tireless advocate of hands-on-science. His website, which contains additional material on slime, can be accessed at www.chymist.com.

I owe a debt of gratitude to Robert Becker, chemistry teacher extraordinaire at Kirkwood High School in Kirkwood, Missouri, for carefully reviewing this manuscript. Robert made numerous helpful suggestions as to content and wording. His technical expertise and keen eye for detail have made this a much better book. Robert is one of the country's foremost innovators in chemical education. He is a much sought after speaker and workshop presenter at science teacher conferences. He has dazzled audiences for years with his spectacular chemistry demonstrations and many creative methods of teaching science. He is the author of *20 Demonstrations Guaranteed to Knock Your Socks Off: Vol. I & II*. His ideas have revolutionized the way that I, and many others, teach science.

Thanks also to Steve Spangler of Steve Spangler Science for reviewing this book and offering many encouraging comments.

A special thanks to Jim Haskins for providing all of the illustrations. Jim is an aspiring young artist who is a former student of mine. I deeply appreciate all of his hard work as well as his creative flair.

Thanks to Frank Reuter, who made the final edit of the manuscript. He offered numerous suggestions that have greatly improved the overall readability of this book.

Finally, I would like to thank my wife Lisa for putting up with a kitchen that was transformed into a slime laboratory during the writing of this book. She has patiently endured countertops full of various slime concoctions for months on end and graciously dealt with the continual exhaustion of supplies from her kitchen cupboard as I sought to perfect the newest slime recipe.

TABLE OF CONTENTS

Part II: Incredible Edible Slime

INTRODUCTION

I have yet to meet a child who does not enjoy making slime. The process of making something that will ooze between your fingers and change shape right before your eyes is innately fascinating. My students, both young and old, invariably get excited when given a chance to make slime. Most teachers I know have one or two varieties of slime that they make with their students. Yet so many other types of slime—at least 50!— can be made, all of which illustrate important scientific principles.

Pure Slime is designed to make science come alive with easy-to-do, readily understandable experiments that use only household substances. The procedure for making each variety of slime is presented in a step-by-step fashion. And most importantly, the science behind the slime is discussed for each experiment.

Many of the slime experiments included in this book have been around for a while. A few of the recipes will be familiar to those who have made slime before. But in addition to the classic slime formulas, many new variations never before published have been added. I have painstakingly tried to locate the original source of each slime recipe that is not my own and have compiled an extensive list of references at the end of this book. These references should prove helpful for those desiring to do further research into any area of slime science.

The experiments in this book will provide hours of fun and learning for kids (and adults!) of all ages. Most of the experiments are suitable for grades K–12 as long as competent adult supervision is present. Young children can learn important skills such as following directions, measuring, pouring, and manipulating substances with their hands. Older students can learn about the chemical processes that go into making slime. Some might even become entrepreneurs and market and sell the slime they make. Whatever your motivation, making slime is sure to be both enjoyable and educational.

WHAT IS SLIME?

According to Webster's Dictionary, slime can be defined in the following ways:

- soft, moist earth, having an adhesive quality
- viscous mud
- any soft, ropy, glutinous, or viscous substance
- a mucous, viscous substance exuded from the bodies of certain animals
- any moist or sticky substance that is considered filthy and disgusting
- in mining, ore reduced to a fine powder, forming a kind of ore mud

Most of the above qualities do not pertain to the slime you will make (especially the part about slime being filthy and disgusting!) However, most varieties of slime are very viscous. Viscosity is defined as resistance to flow. Thicker liquids, like molasses, are more viscous than thinner liquids like water. Ideally, slime should not be too runny or too thick, and should definitely not stick to your hands when you play with it. Most of your slimes will be viscous substances that appear to be a cross between a solid and a liquid. Other types of slime will turn into elastic solids.

Viscosity is measured in units known as centipoise (cps). The chart on the following page shows the relative viscosity of several different substances. Most of your slimes will be more viscous than ketchup, but less viscous than peanut butter. As you make the various types of slime in this book, compare their viscosity with that of the substances on this chart.

Substance	Viscosity in cps at 21°C (70°F)
Acetone	.3
Water	1–5
Blood, kerosene	10
Antifreeze	15
Corn oil, SAE 10 motor oil	50–100
Maple syrup, SAE 30 motor oil	150–200
Castor oil, SAE 40 motor oil	250–500
Glycerin	1,000–2,000
Karo® corn syrup, honey	2,000–3,000
Blackstrap molasses	5,000–10,000
Hershey's® chocolate syrup	10,000–25,000
Heinz® ketchup, French's® mustard	150,000–250,000
Tomato paste, peanut butter	1,000,000–2,000,000
Crisco® shortening, lard	5,000,000–10,000,000
Window putty	100,000,000

To understand how slime behaves, it is necessary to examine some of the theories of Isaac Newton. Isaac Newton (1642–1727) is best known for formulating his revolutionary theories of motion and gravitation. In his spare time, he even invented an advanced form of mathematics known as calculus! But Newton also proposed a simple model of fluids that most common liquids, such as water and oil, obey. His model states that the viscosity of fluids do not change when pressure is applied to them. According to Newton, the only way to change the viscosity of a liquid is to change its temperature. Cooling a liquid makes it more viscous, and heating a liquid makes it less viscous, hence the expression "slower than molasses in January."

Certain types of fluids, however, do not obey Newton's model. These fluids are called non-Newtonian fluids.

Most types of slime, as well as a few other liquids, fall into this category. Their viscosity can be changed by factors other than temperature—such as agitation or pressure. A slime purist would most likely consider only non-Newtonian fluids to be slime, but we are using a broader definition of slime in this book.

If the viscosity of a fluid **increases with increased pressure**, that fluid is termed rheopectic. These substances are also referred to as shear thickening. They become thicker when they undergo a shear stress. A shear stress is defined as any force imparted to a liquid that causes movement, such as stirring, pouring, squeezing, or spreading. Most types of slime, such as Silly Putty® and cornstarch in water, are rheopectic, as is peanut butter. Quicksand is a good example of a rheopectic substance. If you were to fall into quicksand, the more you struggle the more it would grab you, since it becomes more viscous as you thrash about in it.

The synovial fluid in the joints of your knees and elbows is another example of a rheopectic fluid. It is usually not very viscous, allowing for easy movement of the joints. But if a sudden stress is applied to the joint, such as from a sharp twist or a hit from a powerful force, this fluid will instantly become much more viscous. As a result, the joint is cushioned and protected from damage.

Other types of non-Newtonian fluids are thixotropic. The viscosity of thixotropic fluids **decreases as the pressure is increased**. These substances are also referred to as shear thinning. They become thinner when they undergo a shear stress. Some common thixotropic substances are margarine, ketchup, gelatin solutions, mayonnaise, honey, mustard, shaving cream, and Elmer's® glue. A further example would be the need to whack the bottom of a ketchup bottle to get the ketchup to come out. The ketchup becomes less viscous (more runny) when a stress is applied to it, making it easier to pour from the bottle.

The viscosity of non-Newtonian fluids is time dependent. If a thixotropic fluid remains undisturbed for a time, it will become **more** viscous, such as a bottle of ketchup. If a rheopectic fluid remains undisturbed for a time, it will become **less** viscous and may flow into a puddle, such as Silly Putty®.

The various types of slime you make in this book will generally fall into one of these three categories: Newtonian, rheopectic, or thixotropic. As you make them and experiment with them, see if you can determine which category each type of slime falls into.

Most of the slimes you make will be examples of polymers. A polymer is composed of giant chains of molecules composed of repeating units known as monomers. The prefix poly- means many. In some polymers, such as polyethylene, the monomers are all identical. In others, such as proteins, the monomers may vary. A single polymer molecule may be composed of hundreds of thousands of monomers bonded together. Polymers may be natural—such as starch, protein, cellulose, and rubber. Or they may be synthetic—such as plastic, nylon, and Silly Putty®.

The natural world has many types of slime. Algae— plant-like protists—are very slimy. They can be found growing on the sides of aquariums or floating on the surface of ponds. Algae are often referred to as pond scum. Many types of algae are referred to as seaweed, and we will use seaweed in one of our slime recipes.

Another type of natural slime is slime mold. Slime molds resemble fungi, but are actually a type of protist. (The protist kingdom contains organisms that do not quite fit into the other four kingdoms—bacteria, fungi, plants, and animals. They often appear to share characteristics of both plants and animals.) Slime molds are often brightly colored, usually yellow or orange. They grow and advance along the ground just like a fungus. They have both a very slimy feel and appearance. Slime molds feed on dead and rotting plant material just as fungi do, but they can also feed on living organisms as well.

The list of slimy animals is quite long. Slugs, snails, frogs, salamanders, fish, oysters, and earthworms all exhibit varying degrees of sliminess.

In your body, slime is essential for survival. A slimy substance known as mucus is secreted by mucous membranes within your body. Your stomach is lined with mucus, which prevents it from being digested by its own stomach acid. Mucous membranes line the respiratory tubes leading to your lungs, preventing dust and other particles from entering. When you have a cold, your nose may run with a slimy type of mucus that is often referred to as snot. You will even make a type of slime that very closely resembles snot!

It is a very slimy world, after all. And you are about to make it much slimier.

THE SCIENCE BEHIND THE SLIME

Pure Slime is first and foremost a science book. The most important part of doing any experiment is developing an understanding of **why** things happen. Science is built upon the work of men and women who always asked why when observing the world around them. Listed below are just some of the science concepts covered in this book. You will surely discover many more.

- **Physical and chemical changes.** Sometimes slime is produced by a chemical change; other times it is the product of a physical change.
- **Solubility and the nature of mixtures.** Many types of slime are made from solutions. Other types of slime are made from gels, which are examples of colloids.
- **Atomic structure.** The nature of matter, atoms, and molecules is frequently discussed.
- **Polymers.** Most types of slime are polymers, which make up much of our synthetic and natural world.
- **Non-Newtonian fluids.** Many types of slime do not follow the normal behavior of most fluids.
- **Viscosity.** An understanding of this important characteristic of fluids is essential to understanding how slime behaves.
- **Science of cooking.** Many of the principles used in slime-making also apply to recipes used in the kitchen.

- **Fluorescence and phosphorescence.** In discussing fluorescent and glow-in-the-dark slime, the principles of electron excitation and light emission are incorporated.
- **Phases of matter.** The properties of liquids and solids is a recurring theme in this book.
- **Acids and bases.** The pH scale and the properties of acids and bases are discussed.
- **Recycling.** The recycling of certain plastics and paper is examined.

A BRIEF HISTORY OF SLIME

Probably the very first synthetic slime ever developed was Silly Putty®. It was first created in 1943 by a scientist from General Electric named James Wright, during the height of World War II. (This was the same year that steel pennies were made, in order to conserve copper for the war effort.) Since rubber was in such high demand during the war, the search was on to find a rubber substitute. By mixing silicone oil, boric acid, and other substances, an amazing new polymer was discovered. It could be pulled, stretched, deformed, and bounced. Yet it was worthless as a rubber substitute.

The as yet unnamed Silly Putty® sat on a shelf until 1949, when a toy shop owner was given a piece of this amazing substance at a party. Her advertising consultant, Peter Hodgson, made history when he entered it in the 1950 International Toy Fair in New York City. After a mention in "The Talk of the Town" feature of *The New Yorker* shortly afterward, a quarter-of-a-million orders were received within 3 days. Since then, over 300 million individual pieces of Silly Putty® have been sold. If put together, it would form a mass larger than the Goodyear Blimp! When Peter Hodgson died in 1976, he left a $140 million estate.

Silly Putty® has been chemically analyzed, revealing the following composition:
- 65% Dimethyl siloxane hydroxy-terminated polymers with boric acid
- 17% Silica, quartz crystalline
- 9% Thixotrol ST
- 4% Polydimethylsiloxane (silicone oil)
- 1% Decamethyl cyclopentasiloxane

- 1% Glycerine
- 1% Titanium dioxide

However, knowing what something is made of and knowing how to make it are two different things. We know the exact chemical composition of the human body, but to date no one has ever been able to make one. Since Silly Putty® has never been patented, the exact way to synthesize it has never been revealed. Therefore, anyone could manufacture it and call it by a different name . . . if they could figure out how to make it.

Since the advent of Silly Putty®, many other types of slime have been commercially created. Numerous concoctions of varying degrees of viscosity have been successfully marketed under names such as Slime®, Gak®, Floam®, Gak Splat®, Mars Mud®, Blobz®, Gooze®, Skweeez®, and many more.

Probably the first book ever written about slime was *Bartholomew and the Oobeleck*, written by Theodor Geisel (aka Dr. Seuss) in 1949. In this classic children's tale, the king of Didd orders his royal magicians to make something new fall from the sky. The next day huge blobs of green, gooey oobeleck rain down on the kingdom. If not for the wisdom of the page boy Bartholomew, the entire kingdom would have been flooded with this slimy substance.

Many teachers today still refer to the slime they make with their kids as oobeleck. Even though the word *slime* is never mentioned in the book, oobeleck clearly shares many curious properties with slime as we know it today. It flows like a liquid but is still elastic. It can be stretched out, yet it always snaps back to its original shape.

Slime has played a starring role in several feature films. The 1984 smash hit *Ghostbusters*, starring Bill Murray and Dan Akroyd, centers around a team of paranormal exterminators. The ghosts always leave behind a slimy substance termed "ectoplasmic residue." A ghostly encounter always ends with the victim being slimed.

In 1997, Walt Disney released a remake of the classic 1961 movie *The Absent-Minded Professor*, starring Fred MacMurray. The new movie was called *Flubber*, and it starred Robin Williams as the absent-minded professor. He synthesizes a green, highly elastic, viscous elastomer that he terms "Flubber"—short for flying rubber. The amazing thing about Flubber is that if you apply a small amount of energy to it, it liberates a tremendous amount of energy. Unfortunately, this violates the First Law of Thermodynamics which states that energy can neither be created nor destroyed. You cannot receive more energy from a substance than you put into it. Despite this scientific shortcoming, it is still a worthwhile movie.

Most kids today are familiar with the Nickelodeon feature known as *Slime Time*, where participants are doused with gallons of green slime. Disgusting as it may appear, kids seem to greatly enjoy being slimed!

SLIME SAFETY

In order to ensure a safe and fun slime experience, please observe all of the following safety precautions when doing the experiments in this book:

- All experiments are to be done only under competent adult supervision.
- Do not taste or drink any of the slime produced in the *Incredible Inedible Slime* section of the book.
- Keep slime away from small children and pets, who may be tempted to put it in their mouths.
- Never inhale any chemical substance. To determine the odor of a substance, wave your hand over the opening of the container and gently waft the fumes towards your nose.
- Always wear safety goggles when doing any experiment.
- Always have a fire extinguisher nearby when using open flames.
- If a toxic or corrosive chemical spills on your skin, immediately wash it off with copious amounts of water.
- If a chemical splashes in your eyes, rinse them thoroughly with water for 15 minutes and seek medical attention immediately.
- Always read the label of any chemical thoroughly before using.
- Dispose of any chemical only according to the instructions on the label.
- Store all hazardous chemicals out of the reach of children.

- Keep all flammable materials away from open flames.
- If you have long hair, tie it back when working around open flames.
- Do not wear loose-fitting or baggy clothing when working with open flames or chemicals.
- Do not pour any slime products down the drain. They may cause your drain to become clogged.
- Wear old clothes when working with slime.
- Keep slime away from carpets and furniture. It may cause permanent stains and will be difficult to remove from fabrics.
- Always discard any slime if mold develops on it.
- Any former food or beverage containers (such as 2-Liter bottles) should have their labels removed and be clearly marked as to their contents if used to store slime or other substances.
- When heating any substance in the microwave oven, exercise caution as superheating may occur. If a superheated liquid is moved or disturbed in any way, it may erupt violently.
- Wash hands thoroughly when finished making or playing with slime.

SLIME TIPS

Making slime is not always an exact science. Sometimes slime seems to have a mind of its own. The following tips should help you to produce the very best slime . . . most of the time.

- If the slime is too runny, you have several options. Try beginning again with a little less liquid. You can also let the concoction sit overnight or put it in the refrigerator for a while.
- If the slime is too sticky, rinse it with water. If the slime is still sticky, work it with your hands until it no longer leaves a residue. As a last resort, put a little talcum powder (baby powder) on your hands and work it into the slime.
- If the slime is too thick, begin again with a little more liquid.
- Always add food coloring and mix it in thoroughly before you start adding the other ingredients to make your slime.
- Feel free to vary the amounts of substances used in order to achieve the consistency of slime you desire.
- If a slime recipe does not seem to be working, it could be due to impurities in your tap water. Try again using distilled water.
- To prevent slime from drying out, dip it in water before storing.
- Always store slime in an airtight zip-lock bag to prevent it from drying out.

- Store organic slimes in the refrigerator to prolong their shelf life. Always clearly label the container before placing it in the refrigerator.
- Discarded plastic film canisters make excellent storage receptacles for your slime. They are usually available free of charge from any store that processes film for developing.

SLIME STUFF

The following is a master list of all lab apparatus and materials used in this book:

Lab apparatus:
- 20 oz plastic soda bottles
- 2-Liter bottles
- Baby food jars
- Balance
- Balloons
- Beakers or microwave-safe containers
- Black light
- Blender
- Bowls
- Cake pans
- Candy thermometer
- Coffee filters
- Cookie sheet
- Disposable transparent plastic cups
- Eyedroppers
- Film canisters
- Funnels
- Large stirring spoons
- Laser pointer
- Measuring cups
- Measuring spoons (teaspoons and tablespoons)
- Metal soup can
- Microwave oven
- Miscellaneous jars
- Narrow-mouthed glass jars
- Oven mitts or potholders

- Pans or beakers
- Plastic sandwich bags
- Pliers
- Popsicle sticks
- Refrigerator/freezer
- Ruler
- Saucepan
- Scissors
- Small aluminum pie pans
- Stove or other heat source
- Styrofoam® cups
- Thread
- Tornado Tube® (available in toy stores)
- Wax paper
- Window screen mounted on a frame (a screen used to put over aquariums works very well; you can also make your own by nailing some screening material over a frame made with boards)
- Wooden spoon
- Zip-lock storage or freezer bags (quart-size)

Materials:
- 20 Mule Team Borax® (available in grocery stores)
- Acetone (available in hardware stores; also found in some brands of fingernail polish remover)
- Ammonia
- Applesauce
- Arrowroot powder (available in health food stores or from CedarVale Natural Health, Inc. at 866-758-1012 or www.cedarvale. net)
- Baking soda (sodium bicarbonate)
- Butter

- Calcium chloride (available in hardware and grocery stores as an ice melter; sometimes labeled as Driveway Heat™)
- Chocolate syrup
- Cinnamon
- Clear Gel® food thickener (available in restaurant supply stores or food specialty stores; it can also be purchased online at http://www.bluechip group. net/ products/instantclearjel. htm)
- Cornstarch
- Cream of tartar
- Creamy peanut butter
- Dish soap
- Disposable diapers
- Disposable polyvinyl alcohol laundry bags (available from a hospital or medical supply store)
- Distilled water
- Elmer's® Glue Gel (or a comparable blue glue gel)
- Elmer's® white glue (or equivalent)
- Ethyl alcohol (available in hardware and drug stores, as denatured alcohol)
- Flour
- Fluorescent highlighter
- Food coloring
- Friendly Plastic® beads (available in art supply stores; also available from Jewelry Supply in Roseville, CA at 916-780-9610 or www.jewelbay. com /EJS/ friendlyplasticsindex.htm)
- Gaviscon® liquid antacid (available in drug stores)
- Glow-in-the dark paint or medium (available in craft and hobby shops; also available from Glow Inc. at 410-551-4874 or www.hobbyglow.com)

- Guar gum powder (available in health food stores or from CedarVale Natural Health, Inc. at 866-758-1012 or www.cedarvale.net/herbs/guar gum powder.htm)
- Gum arabic (available in art supply stores in solution form; available in powder form from CedarVale Natural Health, Inc. at 866-758-1012 or www.cedarvale. net)
- Gummi® Bears
- Heavy whipping cream
- Honey
- Light corn syrup
- Liquid hand soap containing glycol stearate, not glycol distearate (some, but not all, brands of Softsoap® will work)
- Liquid latex (used for making molds—available in craft and hobby shops)
- Liquid laundry starch
- Metamucil® (available in drug stores)
- Mineral oil (available in drug stores)
- Mustard
- Newspapers
- Nonfat dry milk
- Oil of peppermint
- Oil-free moisturizing lotion
- Plain tapioca
- Powdered pectin (available in grocery and department stores—look in the canning supplies)
- PVA acid-free bookbinding glue (available in art supply stores or directly from the manufacturer Books By Hand, at www.BooksByHand.com or 505-255-3534)
- Regular gelatin dessert (blue and red)

- Skim milk
- Sodium polyacrylamide crystals (available in garden centers as Soil Moist®—used to keep plants moist during times of drought)
- Sodium silicate solution (available in hardware and drug stores, in the paint section)
- Soft, reusable freezer packs (commercially available under various trade names—look in department, grocery, and sporting goods stores)
- Starch packing peanuts (available in office supply stores)
- Sugar-free fruit-flavored gelatin dessert
- Sugarless gum
- Sweetened condensed milk
- Table salt
- Table sugar
- Talcum powder (baby powder)
- Tincture of iodine
- Toothpaste (regular paste, not gel)
- Turmeric (available in grocery stores, in the spice section)
- Unflavored gelatin
- Vanilla extract
- Vegetable oil
- Vinegar
- Washing soda (available in grocery stores in the laundry detergent section)
- White 100% silicone rubber sealant (available in hardware stores)
- White bread

METRIC TO ENGLISH CONVERSIONS

The United States is one of the few countries in the world that has not yet completely converted to the metric system. We still rely heavily on the English system of measurement, which uses arcane units such as miles, gallons, and pounds, instead of the metric units of meters, Liters, and grams. But in the scientific domain the metric system is used almost exclusively. Therefore, we will use the metric system of measurement in this book, with the corresponding English equivalent in parenthesis. Occasionally, a unit conversion will be rounded for simplicity. For example, 237 mL (1 cup) will be rounded to 240 mL throughout this book. The following are some conversions that you may find useful in making slime:

- 1 teaspoon (tsp) = 5 milliliters (mL)
- 3 teaspoons = 1 tablespoon (tbsp)
- 1 tablespoon = 15 mL
- 16 tablespoons = 1 cup
- 1 fluid ounce (fl oz) = 2 tbsp
- 1 fluid ounce = 30 mL
- 1 cup = 8 fl oz
- 1 cup = 240 mL
- 2 cups = 1 pint (pt)
- 2 pints = 1 quart (qt)
- 4 quarts = 1 gallon (gal)
- 1 quart = .946 Liters (L)
- 1 Liter = 1.06 qt
- 16 ounces = 1 pound (lb)
- 1 ounce = 28.4 grams (g)

PART I
INCREDIBLE
INEDIBLE SLIME

You will learn to make forty incredible inedible varieties of slime in the first part of this book, providing you with many hours of fun and scientific inquiry. As the name implies, none of the slime made in the first part of this book should be tasted or eaten. It should also be kept away from pets or small children who may attempt to put it into their mouths. Slime will stain clothing, carpets, and furniture—so be careful. Please follow all safety precautions and always have an adult present when making slime. It is a good idea to record the results of all your experiments in a science journal. You never know what new discoveries you might make. So have fun exploring the incredible inedible world of slime!

Experiment One
THE WORLD'S BEST SLIME!

The very first type of slime you will make is a very durable, stretchy type of slime that can withstand a great deal of abuse. It is a great stress reliever and can provide you with many hours of relaxing fun.

What you need
- Elmer's® white glue (or equivalent)
- 20 Mule Team Borax® (available in grocery stores)
- Food coloring
- 2-Liter bottle
- Eyedropper
- Popsicle stick for stirring
- Zip-lock storage or freezer bag
- Disposable plastic cups
- Narrow-mouthed glass bottle (a Snapple® iced tea bottle is ideal)
- Microwave oven or other heat source
- Microwave-safe container or beaker
- Bowl
- Permanent marker
- Water-based marker

Safety precautions
Adult supervision required. This slime should not be tasted or eaten. Keep it away from young children and pets. Borax is toxic and irritating to the skin and eyes. Wear safety goggles. Exercise caution with boiling water.

How to make it

1. Pour 60 mL (¼ cup) of glue into a plastic cup.
2. Add 60 mL (¼ cup) of water to the glue and stir thoroughly. You now have a 50:50 glue-water mixture. You can make as much or as little slime as you desire, as long as you maintain the 50:50 ratio between the glue and water.
3. Add a few drops of food coloring, if desired, and stir thoroughly.
4. Remove the label from an empty 2-Liter bottle and prominently label as "Borax." Add 120 mL (½ cup) of borax powder to the bottle. Fill halfway with water, and shake vigorously for several minutes. This will form a saturated borax solution. All of the borax will not dissolve right away, but most will dissolve over time. You can use the solution even if all of the solid has not dissolved.
5. Pour 45 mL (3 tbsp) of the borax solution into an empty cup. Using your eyedropper, add this solution a little at a time to the glue-water mixture. The slime will collect on your stick as you stir. It is important that you not add too much borax solution, or the slime will become too stiff. A good rule of thumb is to stop adding borax when there is still a little fluid left in the bottom of the cup. This way, you will avoid adding too much borax.
6. Remove the slime from the stick with your fingers, rinse off with water, and then work it with your hands.

What to do with it

1. Attempt to pull the slime apart slowly. What happens?
2. Now attempt to pull the slime apart rapidly. What happens?
3. Try to bounce it on the floor. Are you successful?
4. Poke it quickly with your finger. What happens?
5. Try to determine if your slime is a solid or a liquid. If left on the table, what happens to its shape? If your slime assumes the shape of its container, does this make it a solid or a liquid?
6. Cut off the bottom half of a 2-L soda bottle and invert it so it acts like a funnel. Prop it up between two stacks of books so it is directly over a cup. Place the slime in the funnel and record the time it takes to reach the cup. Is the flow rate a good indicator of viscosity? Try varying the recipe to see how this affects the flow rate.
7. Place your slime on a newspaper and then press down firmly. (This works best with non-colored slime.) Is the newsprint transferred to the slime? Repeat with other types of print, such as a photocopy. Is the toner transferred? Test a page from an inkjet printer, and then try a page from a laser printer. What happens?
8. Write on a piece of paper with a permanent marker. Press the slime down on the writing. (This works best with non-colored slime.) Is the ink transferred to the slime? Repeat with a water-based marker. What happens?
9. You can design your own colorful slime by drawing on it with markers or paint. Experiment to see what gives you the best results.

10. To demonstrate the fluid-like properties of your slime, try this: Fill a Snapple® bottle (or any narrow-mouthed glass bottle) to the brim with boiling water. Using a potholder to hold the bottle, pour out the boiling water. Quickly place a ball of slime on top of the bottle. Press it down a little so it makes a tight seal. Plunge the bottle into a bowl of cold water and observe the slime. It appears to get "sucked" into the bottle!

11. Try blowing slime bubbles! Wrap the slime around the end of a straw, then blow gently and slowly through the other end. It is important that an airtight seal be made between the slime and the straw. With practice, you can blow slime bubbles the size of a basketball!

12. Store the slime in a zip-lock bag.

The science behind the slime

Elmer's® glue is primarily composed of the polymer polyvinyl acetate. It has a greater viscosity (resistance to flow) than many liquids, but is not nearly as viscous as slime. The borax solution causes the polyvinyl acetate molecules to become crosslinked. Crosslinking can be compared to the placement of wooden ties to hold the rails of a railroad track in place. The borax (sodium tetraborate) molecules dissolve in water to produce borate ions $(B(OH)_4^-)$. These borate ions act like the ties, which hold the rails of the polyvinyl acetate molecules in place. This makes for a much more viscous solution, since the polyvinyl acetate molecules are now linked firmly together by the borate ions. (See diagrams on next page.)

Fig. 1. Since these polymer chains are not crosslinked, they slide freely past one another, producing a substance of low viscosity.

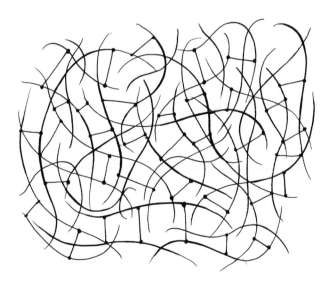

Fig. 2. Crosslinking of the polymer chains restricts their freedom of movement, producing a substance of high viscosity.

Slime is an example of a non-Newtonian fluid. According to Isaac Newton, the viscosity of a liquid is dependent only on its temperature. But the viscosity of a non-Newtonian fluid, such as slime, can be altered in several other ways besides changing its temperature. If you pull the slime slowly apart, it will form long thin strands. But if pulled apart rapidly, it breaks. It can bounce somewhat if formed into a ball and dropped on a hard surface. If poked quickly with a finger, the finger will bounce off. But if poked slowly with a finger, the slime can easily be deformed. Other examples of non-Newtonian fluids are quicksand and Silly Putty®.

Since the slime will assume the shape of its container, it is considered to be a liquid, not a solid. Solids have a definite shape; liquids do not. However, the slime is a very slow-flowing liquid, which is classified as one having a high degree of viscosity.

Water-based ink will tend to be more easily transferred to the slime than permanent ink. Water-based ink will also tend to run when used to draw on slime, but permanent ink will tend to make a more lasting impression.

When the bottle full of boiling water is emptied, the air within the bottle is heated. As air is heated, it expands. This expansion of hot air forces some of the air out of the bottle. When the bottle is cooled, the air within the bottle is cooled as well. When air cools, it contracts. Since some of the air was forced out of the bottle earlier, after cooling there is now less air pressure inside the bottle than there is outside the bottle. As a result, the slime is pushed into the bottle by this greater outside air pressure. It is important to note that the slime was pushed into the bottle, not sucked—remember, science never sucks! This experiment vividly demonstrates that slime is a liquid, which can be molded to fit into its container.

Fun fact: Borax deposits were discovered in Death Valley, California in 1881. The brand name *20 Mule Team Borax*® comes from the fact that twenty-mule teams were used to transport it from the mines. Sometimes a team would actually consist of eighteen mules and two horses. (The name *18 Mule and Two Horse Borax* never quite caught on.) The mule teams were replaced by railroad cars in 1889. Not one animal ever died from transporting borax from these mines.

Incredible Inedible Slime
Experiment Two
DIAPER SLIME!

Diaper slime will help you discover why diapers are so absorbent. It is made by extracting the powder from a disposable diaper and then adding water. The result is a very heavy gel that will retain its water indefinitely. (To make your diaper slime more closely resemble the contents of a used diaper, yellow food coloring can be added.)

What you need
- Disposable diaper
- Transparent plastic cup
- Distilled water
- Salt
- Scissors
- Popsicle stick for stirring
- Zip-lock bag
- Cookie sheet

Safety precautions
Adult supervision required. The diaper slime should not be tasted or eaten. Keep it away from young children and pets. Sodium polyacrylate is toxic if ingested. Wash hands after handling. Do not allow this material to go down the drain.

How to make it
1. Using scissors, carefully cut away the inner lining of a diaper.

2. Attempt to remove as much of the powder as possible, by shaking the diaper onto a cookie sheet. (It may be necessary to shake out some of the fibers as well in order to remove the powder.) The powder that falls out is sodium polyacrylate. Add this powder to a cup.
3. Slowly add distilled water and observe as a gel forms. How much water does the powder absorb?

What to do with it

1. After adding a little water, attempt to hold the cup upside down. Hopefully, the diaper slime will not fall out!
2. You can perform a great little magic trick if you can obtain about a teaspoon of pure sodium polyacrylate. Place this substance in an opaque cup ahead of time, and add a little water so the powder will stay in the cup without falling out when turned upside-down. Have two other empty cups nearby. Initially place all the cups upside-down. Now place each cup right-side-up and in front of your audience add about a half-cup of water to the cup containing the sodium polyacrylate. Mix up the order of your cups and then ask your audience to identify the cup with the water. Turn each cup upside down. The water will have "magically" disappeared!
3. Add a couple of teaspoons of salt to the diaper slime and stir. What happens?
4. Make up some fresh diaper slime in a clear cup. Add some radish seeds. Observe over a time period of several weeks.

5. Immerse a second whole diaper in water for about a minute. Remove the diaper and dissect it with a pair of scissors. What do you observe?

6. Store the slime in a zip-lock bag.

The science behind the slime

If you have ever put a diaper-clad baby in a swimming pool, you have already seen firsthand the amazing superabsorbent properties of diapers. All disposable diapers contain a superabsorbent polymer known as sodium polyacrylate, which is capable of absorbing 800 times its weight in pure water, 300 times its weight in tap water, and 60 times its weight in salt water. Since urine is salty, sodium polyacrylate cannot absorb as much urine as fresh water.

The powder you removed from the diaper is what makes the diaper so absorbent. Only a very small amount is needed. A very large diaper may contain up to 12 grams of superabsorbent powder, with smaller diapers containing less. When the diaper is dissected, you can observe the powder absorbing water to form a gel.

Salt will draw water from the gel, causing it to turn back into a liquid. When salt is added to the gel, it forms a very concentrated solution of salt water on the surface of the gel. The concentration of water is now much greater within the gel than on its surface. Therefore, water will diffuse out of the gel until the concentration of water both within and outside of the gel is equal. As a result, the structure of the gel is destroyed and its viscosity decreases dramatically.

Pure sodium polyacrylate can be obtained from magic and novelty shops, or science supply stores. If a teaspoon of this powder is added to an empty cup, a full cup of water can then be poured in, creating an instant gel. You can then turn the cup upside-down and it will not fall out! Magicians sometimes use this powder to make water "disappear."

A crosslinked form of sodium polyacrylate has been used to make artificial snow. It is marketed under various names, such as PolySnow™ or Insta-Sno™, and it looks just like the powder in the diaper. When water is added, however, it puffs up to instantly form a fluffy white substance that looks just like snow. The powder can absorb up to 500 times its weight in water. It has been used on ski slopes and also on movie sets. To find out where to obtain this product, do a web search on the Internet for PolySnow™ or Insta-Sno™.

Sodium polyacrylate has recently been marketed as a substance called Barricade®, which is used to prevent the spread of fires. When spread over the surface of a wall or roof, saturated sodium polyacrylate provides an excellent barrier to the spread of fire. It has also been used to stop the spread of forest fires. This application was first suggested by firefighters who noticed that wet diapers would not burn.

Fun fact: Proctor and Gamble introduced Pampers®, the first disposable diaper, in 1961. Sodium polyacrylate was not added to the disposable diaper until 1984. This innovation made diapers thinner, more leakproof, and about 50% lighter.

Incredible Inedible Slime
Experiment Three
GHOST CRYSTAL SLIME!

The slime formed in this experiment is indeed quite slimy, yet will be in the form of individual crystals. These crystals are often called ghost crystals, for reasons that will become apparent.

What you need
- Sodium polyacrylamide crystals (available in garden centers as Soil Moist®—used to keep plants moist during times of drought)
- Zip-lock quart-size freezer bag
- Thread
- Cookie sheet
- Oven

Safety precautions
Adult supervision required. The ghost crystal slime should not be tasted or eaten. Keep it away from young children and pets. Sodium polyacrylamide crystals are harmless to the touch, but can be harmful if swallowed. Do not pour them down the drain.

How to make it
1. Place about 5 mL (1 tsp) of dry ghost crystals into the quart freezer bag. They will be very small and hard.
2. Add about 700 mL (3 cups) of water.

3. Observe them periodically over the next 4–6 hours. What do you see?

What to do with it

1. Take a few crystals out of the bag. How do they feel?
2. Remove a few ghost crystals and place them in a clear cup of water. What do you notice?
3. Make a loop with a piece of thread and place it around a ghost crystal. Suspend the loop in water. What do you see?
4. Stick a toothpick through a ghost crystal and submerge in water. What do you see?
5. Remove a ghost crystal from the water and add salt. What happens?
6. Make some more ghost crystals, except this time use colored water. The food coloring must be added to the water before the ghost crystals are added. You can even make a ghost crystal rainbow by making the ghost crystals red, orange, yellow, green, blue, and violet, and then arranging them in this order in a transparent container.
7. Leave a few ghost crystals exposed to the air for a few days. Do they lose water and return to their original mass?
8. Place a few ghost crystals on a cookie sheet and place in the oven on the lowest temperature setting. Monitor the crystals every few minutes. What happens?
9. Remove the original label from a resealable plastic soda bottle and prominently label as "Ghost Crystals." Store your crystals in the bottle.

The science behind the slime

Ghost crystals receive their name because they appear invisible underwater. Because they are composed almost entirely of water, they have the same index of refraction as water. In other words, these crystals bend or refract light to the same degree that pure water does. As a result, they appear invisible when placed underwater.

These crystals have a wide variety of uses. They are commonly sold in garden centers as a way to moderate the water content in soil. If plants are over watered, the polymer crystals absorb the excess water to prevent "drowning" of the roots. Then, over time the crystals release the water back into the soil to keep the plants from drying out in times of drought. Ghost crstals are even utilized in bath gels and as a medium to store crickets for pet food. They have also been used to draw water from fuel tanks.

Ghost crystals are an example of a superabsorbent polymer and can absorb up to 500 times their weight in water. They are similar in composition to the sodium polyacrylate polymer used in baby diapers. You can calculate how much water a ghost crystal will absorb by weighing a crystal before and then after water is added. Try using distilled water, tap water, and salt water. What type of water do you think will be absorbed the most by the ghost crystals? What type of water do you think will be absorbed the least by the ghost crystals?

Fun fact: Ghost crystals have been sewed into the fabric of headbands. The headbands can be soaked in water before wearing, causing them to absorb a great deal of water. As this water gradually evaporates, the skin of the wearer is cooled.

Incredible Inedible Slime
Experiment Four
QUICKSAND SLIME!

The substance made in this experiment has amazing properties that can change right before your eyes. Its composition is similar to that of quicksand. When pressure is applied its properties completely change. Of all the types of slime, it is one of the easiest to make.

What you need
- One 16 oz (454 g) box of cornstarch
- Bowl
- Large spoon
- Zip-lock bag
- Popsicle stick for stirring

Safety precautions
None

How to make it
1. Add the box of cornstarch and 300 mL (1¼ cups) of water to a large bowl.
2. Mix thoroughly until no dry powder remains.

What to do with it
1. Grab a handful of the substance. It will be very runny.
2. Grab another handful, and then squeeze tightly. It will become very hard! When you stop squeezing, what happens?

3. Attempt to poke the mixture in the bowl very quickly with your finger. Your finger will bounce off.
4. Now poke the mixture very slowly with your finger. You can easily touch the bottom of the bowl.
5. Devise your own experiments with this fascinating substance.
6. Store in a zip-lock bag.
7. For an interesting variation, repeat the experiment, except add equal volumes of cornstarch and baking soda to the water. The result will be a firmer variation of quicksand slime.

The science behind the slime

Cornstarch is an example of a polymer, and is composed of repeating units of glucose ($C_6H_{12}O_6$). However, each monomer in the chain actually has a formula of $C_6H_{10}O_5$, since each glucose molecule loses a water molecule during bonding. Due to extensive hydrogen bonding, the granules of starch readily absorb water, making starch an excellent thickener for gravy and sauces. The starch and water together form an interesting example of a non-Newtonian fluid. Unlike most fluids, the viscosity of this mixture is greatly affected by pressure. As the substance is squeezed, it becomes more viscous (less runny). As the pressure exerted on it decreases, it becomes less viscous (more runny).

Quicksand, which is a mixture of sand and water, is subject to the same principles as cornstarch and water. If you are trapped in quicksand, the more you thrash around, the tighter its hold becomes on you, since sudden movements increase its viscosity. Trying to escape quickly from quicksand is nearly impossible. But if you move slowly through quicksand, its viscosity decreases, making it easier to escape.

Fun fact: If trapped in quicksand, lie flat on your back and spread out your arms until rescued. Quicksand is actually denser than saltwater and you can easily float in it.

Incredible Inedible Slime
Experiment Five
ELECTRIC SLIME!

The slime produced in this experiment will be attracted by an electric field. Its flow can be stopped and started at will, by using a charged balloon. This slime is safe to touch, but is much more fascinating simply to watch.

What you need
- Cornstarch
- Vegetable oil
- Balloon
- Disposable plastic cups
- Popsicle stick for stirring
- Zip-lock bag

Safety precautions
Do not taste or eat the electric slime.

How to make it
1. Add 60 mL (¼ cup) of cornstarch to 120 mL (½ cup) of oil in a disposable plastic cup.
2. Stir thoroughly until the mixture has a uniform consistency.

What to do with it
1. Rub a balloon in your hair. Now slowly pour the oil-cornstarch mixture into another cup. As you are pouring, bring the charged balloon near the stream of fluid. Observe.

2. Store the electric slime in a zip-lock bag.

The science behind the slime

The cornstarch forms a colloidal suspension in the oil. This means the particles are not dissolved, but simply dispersed. The mixture of cornstarch and oil is an example of an electrorheological fluid, which is a fluid where the viscosity is affected by an electric field.

In this particular mixture, the particles of cornstarch are temporarily polarized by the charged balloon. A substance is polarized when the positive charges tend to group together on one side and the negative charges on the other side. These polar particles then tend to line up with one another in a long chain in the presence of the balloon's electric field. This creates a chain of particles that are positive on one side and negative on the other.

As a result, the particles have greater difficulty flowing past one another. This alignment tends to restrict the flow of the oil, making it more viscous. The attraction to the charged balloon is so great that the flow will stop, and streams of the liquid will be deflected toward the balloon.

Electrorheological fluids are sometimes known as smart fluids. Since the viscosity of these fluids can be so quickly reversed, they have a wide range of applications— such as in shock absorbers, brakes, clutches, and hydraulic valves.

Fun fact: A group of fluids closely related to electrorheological fluids are termed magnetorheological fluids. The viscosity of these fluids is affected by a magnetic field. They have so far found their greatest use in the space program, such as in suppressing vibrations during rocket launches. Future applications could perhaps include a type of Braille computer monitor.

Incredible Inedible Slime
Experiment Six
SNOT SLIME!

This slime is one of the slimiest slimes you can make. Making it requires a little patience, but when finished you will have a substance that very closely resembles the mucous that sometimes flows from your nose—more commonly known as snot. With a little green food coloring, the slime will look more realistic.

What you need
- Elmer's® glue
- Liquid laundry starch
- Disposable plastic cups
- Popsicle stick for stirring
- Food coloring
- Zip-lock bag

Safety precautions
Adult supervision required. The snot slime is toxic if ingested. Wear safety goggles. This slime should not be tasted or eaten. Keep it away from young children and pets.

How to make it
1. In a disposable cup, add equal volumes of glue and liquid starch.
2. Add a few drops of food coloring, if desired.
3. Stir for 5–10 minutes.

4. Allow the mixture to stand for another 5–10 minutes.

What to do with it

1. Remove the slime with your fingers. It should have the consistency of snot. Allow it to flow between your fingers.
2. This slime makes an excellent "slime timer." Obtain a commercially available Tornado Tube® and attach together two soda bottles. Add the slime and watch it fall between the two bottles.
3. Store the slime in a zip-lock bag.

The science behind the slime

If you read the label on a container of liquid laundry starch, you will find that it contains, among other things, cornstarch and borax. Starch is an excellent thickener, due to its ability to absorb water. Borax causes crosslinking between the polyvinyl acetate molecules that make up Elmer's® glue (see experiment one). As a result, a viscous substance is produced—which creates an excellent type of slime.

Fun fact: The average person swallows about a Liter of snot per day! Snot is usually clear. If it is green or yellow, you probably have a cold. The color is due to the presence of bacteria and bacterial waste.

Incredible Inedible Slime
Experiment Seven
GREAT BALLS OF SLIME!

This slime is similar to the slime made in the first experiment. But it has a firmer, thicker feel. It is a little more viscous. This slime will readily form into a ball—but will not maintain this shape for long!

What you need
- Elmer's® glue
- Borax solution (see experiment one for instructions on how to prepare)
- Talcum powder
- Oil-free moisturizing lotion
- Disposable plastic cups
- Popsicle stick for stirring
- Food coloring
- Zip-lock bag

Safety precautions
Adult supervision required. This slime should not be tasted or eaten. Keep it away from young children and pets. Borax is toxic and irritating to the skin. Wear safety goggles.

How to make it
1. Add the following to a disposable plastic cup: 10 mL (2 tsp) talcum powder, 10 mL (2 tsp) oil-free moisturizing lotion, 20 mL (4 tsp) Elmer's® glue, and 20 mL (4 tsp) water. Stir thoroughly.

2. Add several drops of food coloring. Stir thoroughly.
3. Add 10 mL (2 tsp) borax solution. Stir thoroughly.
4. Remove the slime with your fingers. Rinse it under water.

What to do with it

1. The slime will be quite sticky at first, but as you continue working it with your hands, it will become less sticky. Store the slime in a zip-lock bag when not using it.
2. Attempt to bounce the slime ball on the floor. Does it bounce?
3. Attempt to pull it apart slowly, then quickly. What happens?
4. See if it will stick to a wall. Will it "walk" down the wall if left undisturbed?

The science behind the slime

The ball of slime that forms is due to the crosslinking of borate ions in the borax with the polyvinyl acetate molecules in the glue. This is the same process that occurred with the slime in experiment one. The addition of the talcum powder and moisturizing lotion gives it a firmer body yet more slippery texture than the slime made from just borax and Elmer's glue. The talcum powder provides additional sites for crosslinking, resulting in a more viscous slime. The ball of slime is a great example of a non-Newtonian fluid, since its viscosity is affected by factors other than temperature.

Fun fact: Elmer's® glue first came on the market in 1947, and is produced by the Borden Company. It was originally sold in 2-ounce bottles with wooden applicators. Today it is the best selling glue in America. Elmer is the husband of Elsie the cow, Borden's official symbol. After Elmer was chosen in 1951 to be the marketing symbol for all of Borden's glue products, sales of Elmer's® glue skyrocketed.

Incredible Inedible Slime
Experiment Eight
POLYSTYRENE SLIME!

In this experiment a moldable type of slime is formed from recycled Styrofoam®, which is made from the polymer polysyrene. Unlike many other types of slime, this slime will eventually harden into whatever shape it is molded.

What you need
- Acetone (available in hardware stores; also found in some brands of fingernail polish remover)
- Small aluminum pie pan
- Styrofoam® cups or Styrofoam® egg cartons
- Popsicle stick for stirring

Safety precautions
Adult supervision required. The polystyrene slime should not be tasted or eaten. Keep it away from young children and pets. Read all warnings on the container of acetone before proceeding. Wear safety goggles. Acetone is very flammable—keep it away from open flames. Inhaling acetone vapors is harmful—do this experiment outdoors or in a well-ventilated area. Acetone is toxic if ingested. Do not allow the acetone to contact your skin. Acetone will also ruin any finished woodwork or varnished surface with which it comes into contact. Wash hands thoroughly when finished with this experiment.

How to make it

1. Fill a small aluminum pie pan halfway with acetone.
2. Place a Styrofoam® cup open-end down into the acetone, and push down gently with the wooden stick.
3. Remove the slime with the stick and rinse it thoroughly with water.

What to do with it

1. After rinsing the slime thoroughly with water, fashion it into whatever shape you desire, such as a ball or some other object.
2. Repeat the above procedure with packing peanuts, egg cartons, or other large pieces of Styrofoam®.

The science behind the slime

The Styrofoam® cup is composed of polystyrene, as evidenced by the recycling code of "6" on the bottom. Polystyrene is a polymer composed of many styrene monomers bonded together. Acetone will cause the cup to collapse, but not dissolve. The acetone breaks some of the bonds that give the cup its shape, but the end result is still polystyrene. The collapsing of the cup is a good example of a physical change, since the chemical composition of the substance is not altered.

Styrofoam® is filled with gas, which enhances its insulating abilities. When the cup is placed in acetone, bubbles can be observed as this gas is being released. This removal of gas greatly reduces the volume of the cup. When it dries, the polystyrene will become rigid and once again maintain its shape.

A similar procedure to the one described in this experiment is used to recycle Styrofoam® and other polystyrene products. The recycled material can then be fashioned into a variety of products. Look for the "6" recycling code to determine if a product may have been made from recycled polystyrene. Not only does recycling conserve natural resources, but it also prevents valuable space from being taken up in landfills. Polystyrene takes a long, long time to break down in the environment.

Fun fact: You can create realistic special effects for your next Halloween party by using the procedure outlined in the above experiment. When Styrofoam® is dipped in acetone and then pulled away, the strands of polystyrene look just like spider webs!

Incredible Inedible Slime
Experiment Nine
PACKING PEANUT SLIME!

The slime formed in this experiment will end up looking like instant mashed potatoes, since the primary component of both is starch. Starch is a polymer, as are most types of slime.

What you need
- Starch packing peanuts (available in office supply stores)
- Disposable plastic cups
- Tincture of iodine
- Popsicle stick for stirring

Safety precautions
Adult supervision required. This slime should not be tasted or eaten. Keep it away from young children and pets. Tincture of iodine is toxic if ingested. Wear safety goggles.

How to make it
1. Place some starch packing peanuts in a cup half-filled with water.
2. Stir until they develop a slimy consistency.

What to do with it
1. Have a contest to see who can fit the most packing peanuts into a cup of water.

2. Add a few drops of tincture of iodine to the slimy mixture that forms. What happens?
3. When finished, pour the mixture down the drain.

The science behind the slime

Starch packing peanuts are an excellent alternative to Styrofoam®, in that they are completely biodegradable, and thus do not take up valuable space in landfills. When puffed up with air, they provide excellent packing material. They do not really dissolve in water, but instead form a thick paste, somewhat like mashed potatoes. The decrease in volume occurs when water collapses the structure of the packing peanuts, allowing the air to be released. The mixture turns black when iodine is added, due to the formation of what is commonly known as the starch-iodine complex.

Fun fact: Starch has been used to make an incredible variety of products. One interesting application is its use in a product called SuperSlurper®, which can absorb 2,000 times its weight in water! It has been used in fuel filters, baby powders, and wound dressings.

Incredible Inedible Slime
Experiment Ten
FLUBBER SLIME!

Flubber slime is very similar to commercially available types of slime. It has a distinct slimy feel that nicely runs between your fingers, yet will not stick to your skin.

What you need
- Disposable polyvinyl alcohol laundry bags. (These bags are available from hospitals or medical supply stores. Alternately, powdered PVA can be used for any experiments requiring the use of PVA. Gradually dissolve 4 g of powdered PVA into 100 mL boiling water to make a 4% solution. Heating the solution in a beaker in a microwave for a few minutes is the best way to get the powdered PVA to dissolve. After each 2–3 minutes of heating, remove the solution and stir. Repeat until the powder has completely dissolved. To locate a supplier for the powdered form, do a search on the Internet for "Polyvinyl Alcohol.")
- Measuring cups
- Popsicle stick for stirring
- Food coloring
- Disposable plastic cups
- Borax solution (see experiment one for instructions on how to prepare)
- Eyedropper
- Microwave oven
- Balance
- Zip-lock bag

Safety precautions

Adult supervision required. This slime should not be tasted or eaten. Keep it away from young children and pets. Exercise caution when boiling water. Borax is toxic and irritating to the skin and eyes. Wear safety goggles.

How to make it

1. Using a balance, record the mass of the disposable PVA bag.
2. For each gram of the bag's mass, add 25 mL (5 tsp) of water to a beaker. For example, if the bag has a mass of 28 grams, add 700 mL (2.9 cups) of water to a beaker (28 x 25). This will make a 4% aqueous solution.
3. Heat the beaker of water to boiling in the microwave oven, and then remove the beaker.
4. Completely unfold the bag and then wad it up and place it in the boiling water.
5. With a popsicle stick, agitate the bag for about 5 minutes or until it has completely dissolved.
6. Place the solution in the microwave oven and again heat to boiling.
7. Remove the beaker from the microwave. Stir thoroughly. If any clumps remain, remove them with a spoon and discard. You now have a 4% aqueous solution of polyvinyl alcohol.
8. Allow the mixture to cool to room temperature. To make slime, pour about 20 mL (4 tsp) of this mixture into a disposable cup.
9. Add a few drops of food coloring if desired.
10. Now add the saturated borax solution a few drops at a time with an eyedropper and stir thoroughly. Slime will begin to form on your stick.

11. Add the borax solution until most of the PVA solution has been turned into slime. Be careful not to add too much borax, or it will be too stiff. A good rule of thumb is to make sure there is always a little liquid left in the bottom of the cup when finished. This way you know you have not added too much borax.
12. Remove the slime with your fingers and work it with your hands.
13. Rinse the slime under water.
14. Store the slime in a zip-lock bag.

What to do with it

1. Compare the viscosity of the slime with that of other liquids by placing equal amounts of each substance on a board and then turning the board at an angle. Record how long it takes each substance to travel the length of the board.
2. Place your slime in the refrigerator for about an hour. How does this affect its viscosity?
3. Have fun playing with your slime—this is one of the most beautiful and enjoyable types of slime you can make.

The science behind the slime

The hot water soluble polyvinyl alcohol bags used in this experiment are widely used in hospitals as a way to minimize handling of soiled or contaminated linen and clothing. The bags can be thrown into the washer along with the laundry, with the bag completely dissolving in the wash! These bags are also used to package concentrated insecticide powders. The bags can simply be dropped into a tank of water, where they will dissolve.

These bags are also used to package dyes, deter-gents, and a host of other products when the manu-facturer wants to minimize human ex-posure. Cold water soluble PVA bags are also made, but these may be more difficult to find.

Polyvinyl alcohol was first synthesized in 1924 by reacting acetic acid with acetylene to form vinyl acetate. The vinyl acetate mole-cules then join with one another to produce long polymer chains of polyvinyl alcohol.

When borax is added to the aqueous polyyinyl alcohol solution, the polymer chains become crosslinked, forming a thick viscous gel. It appears to be a solid at first glance, but is actually a very viscous liquid.

Fun fact: The slime called Flubber in the movie *Flubber* did not actually exist. It was strictly a computer animation, and was actually modeled after a type of hair gel!

Incredible Inedible Slime
Experiment Eleven
RIBBONS OF SLIME!

In this experiment, you will add two colorless liquids and end up pulling a long thread-like ribbon of white slime from the surface where the two liquids meet. This intriguing bit of chemical magic is sure to amaze your friends.

What you need
- 4% aqueous solution of polyvinyl alcohol (see previous experiment for instructions on how to prepare)
- Empty metal soup can
- Acetone (available in hardware stores; also found in some brands of fingernail polish remover)
- Popsicle stick for stirring

Safety precautions
Adult supervision required. This slime should not be tasted or eaten. Keep it away from young children and pets. Wear safety goggles. Do this experiment in a well-ventilated area. Do not inhale vapors of acetone. Acetone is highly flammable—keep it away from open flames. Do not allow acetone to touch your skin. Acetone will also ruin any finished woodwork or varnished surface with which it comes into contact. Wash hands thoroughly after doing this experiment.

How to make it

1. Pour about 20 mL (4 tsp) of acetone into an empty soup can.
2. Slowly pour 20 mL (4 tsp) of 4% polyvinyl alcohol solution into the acetone. A white mass will form.

What to do with it

1. With your stirring stick, pull up gently on the white mass. You will be able to lift out a long, elastic ribbon of white slime, which resembles a thick piece of thread.
2. Rinse the ribbon of slime thoroughly with water. Is it still elastic?
3. Place the ribbon of slime on a paper towel and let it dry out overnight. What happens to it?

The science behind the slime

The white mass that forms when the two substances are mixed is solid polyvinyl alcohol (PVA) that has come out of solution. PVA is soluble in water but not in acetone. The water within the PVA solution is attracted to the acetone, but the PVA is not. Therefore the PVA precipitates out of solution as a white solid mass. This solid strand is very elastic, and can be pulled into a long thin ribbon. When it dries out, it loses its elasticity.

Fun fact: Polyvinyl alcohol was first synthesized in 1924. It is a polymer, but it is not made from vinyl alcohol. Vinyl alcohol does not even exist!

Incredible Inedible Slime
Experiment Twelve
GLUE GEL SLIME!

Elmer's® Glue Gel is gaining popularity as the glue of choice among children. Its cool blue color and ease of application make it fun to use. This glue also makes fantastic slime, as you are about to discover.

What you need
- Elmer's® Glue Gel (or a comparable blue glue gel)
- Borax solution (see experiment one for instructions on how to prepare)
- 2-Liter bottle
- Eyedropper
- Disposable plastic cups
- Popsicle stick for stirring
- Food coloring (optional)
- Zip-lock bag

Safety precautions
Adult supervision required. This slime should not be tasted or eaten. Keep it away from young children and pets. Borax is poisonous if ingested and is an eye irritant. Wear safety goggles.

How to make it
1. Add some Elmer's® Glue Gel to a plastic cup. Use as much or as little as you would like.
2. Measure out the same volume of water, and add it to the glue. Stir thoroughly with the popsicle stick. You will now have a 50:50 mixture of glue and

water. At this point, you may add a few drops of food coloring if you wish.

3. Add the saturated borax solution a few drops at a time with an eyedropper until the slime forms on your stick. Continue to stir.

4. Add the borax solution until most of the glue has been turned into slime. Be careful not to add too much borax, or the slime will be too stiff. A good rule of thumb is to make sure there is always a little liquid left in the bottom of the cup when finished. This way you will avoid adding too much borax.

5. Remove the slime with your fingers and work it with your hands.

6. Rinse the slime under water.

7. Store the slime in a zip-lock bag.

What to do with it

1. You can perform the same experiments with this slime that you did with the slime in experiment one.

2. Devise an experiment to compare the viscosity of this slime with that of other types of slime made so far. What do you discover?

3. Make a second batch of slime, except this time add no water to the glue gel. How does this batch differ from the first?

4. For a glittery slime, repeat the experiment with Elmer's® Galactic Glue™, which is very similar to the blue glue gel except that it contains glitter.

The science behind the slime

Elmer's® Glue Gel is an example of a thixotropic gel. In such a substance, the viscosity changes when the molecules are disrupted. If the substance is disturbed, it becomes less viscous (more runny). When the glue bottle is squeezed, it acts more like a liquid and flows out of the bottle. When at rest, it acts more like a solid.

Elmer's Glue Gel is a solution of polyvinyl alcohol in water. The glue also contains many other additives in small amounts. The polyvinyl alcohol molecules tend to slide past one another fairly easily. When the borax is added, it causes the polyvinyl alcohol molecules to become crosslinked. This gives the material its unique slimy texture. You can think of crosslinking as railroad ties which link together two rails—the ties hold the rails in place.

> **Fun fact:** The ancient Greek word for glue was *kolloid*. Most types of glues are colloids, which are suspensions of very fine particles. The huge surface area of these tiny suspended particles helps to give glue its stickiness.

Incredible Inedible Slime
Experiment Thirteen
PUTTY SLIME!

No childhood would be complete without Silly Putty®. This commercially available substance has entertained child and adult alike for years. In this experiment, you will make a type of slime that is similar to Silly Putty®.

What you need
- PVA acid-free bookbinding glue (available from art supply stores or directly from the manufacturer Books By Hand, at www.BooksByHand.com or 505-255-3534)
- Borax solution (see experiment one for instructions on how to prepare)
- Eyedropper
- Disposable plastic cups
- Food coloring
- Zip-lock bag
- Popsicle stick for stirring

Safety precautions
Adult supervision required. This slime should not be tasted or eaten. Keep it away from young children and pets. Borax is toxic and irritating to the skin and eyes. Wear safety goggles.

How to make it
1. Pour some PVA glue into a disposable cup. You can use as much or as little as you like.

2. Add the borax solution a few drops at a time with the eyedropper. Stir after adding.
3. Continue adding borax solution until most of the liquid has turned into slime. The slime will adhere to the stick.
4. Quit adding borax when there is still a little liquid left in the bottom of the cup. This will ensure that you do not add too much borax.
5. Remove the slime from the stick and rinse with water.

What to do with it

1. As you work the slime with your hands, it will become less sticky. Continue to play with the slime until it is no longer sticky.
2. Pull it, stretch it, bounce it, and generally have fun with this amazing Silly Putty® imitation.
3. Store the slime in a zip-lock bag when finished playing with it.

The science behind the slime

The PVA glue contains polyvinyl acetate (PVA). This pH-neutral glue is used for bookbinding and other art projects. Acid-free glue will prevent deterioration of paper products that can occur if the glue is not pH neutral.

The borate ions within the borax causes crosslinking between the polyvinyl acetate molecules, forming a thick viscous mass. Since the PVA molecules can no longer slide past one another with ease, a great type of slime is formed.

Fun fact: Silly Putty® was used by the astronauts during Apollo 8 to keep their tools from floating around in the near zero gravity environment of their spaceship.

Incredible Inedible Slime
Experiment Fourteen
WORM SLIME!

In this experiment, you will make a highly unusual variety of slime that resembles long, narrow worms. Although some varieties of worms are actually edible, this particular variety of worm is not!

What you need
- Gaviscon® liquid antacid (available in drug stores)
- Calcium chloride (available in hardware and grocery stores as an ice melter—sometimes labeled as Driveway Heat™)
- Popsicle stick for stirring
- Disposable plastic cups

Safety precautions
Adult supervision required. This slime should not be tasted or eaten. Keep it away from young children and pets. Wear safety goggles. Calcium chloride is poisonous and will cause eye irritation. Gaviscon® antacid should be stored out of reach of children. Do not pour the worm slime down the drain.

How to make it
1. Prepare an aqueous solution of calcium chloride by adding 5 mL (1 tsp) of calcium chloride to 240 mL (1 cup) of water. Stir until all is dissolved. (A 1% solution is sufficient.)

2. Slowly pour a little Gaviscon® liquid antacid into the calcium chloride solution. Observe.

What to do with it

1. You can take out the polymer worms and note their slimy feel.
2. This experiment provides a great way to test fruit drinks for calcium. Add liquid Gaviscon® to calcium-fortified cranberry or orange juice. The polymer worms will be formed. They will not form in a drink without calcium. Do not drink the juice after Gaviscon® has been added.

The science behind the slime

Sodium alginate (often known as algin) is derived from kelp, which is a large brown type of seaweed. Algin is an example of a polymer, and contains many units of sugar that are linked together to form a polysaccharide (poly- means many and saccharide means sugar). It is one of the inactive ingredients found in liquid Gaviscon®, and is used as both a thickener and an emulsifier. An emulsifier is used to keep substances mixed together that would otherwise settle out.

Sodium alginate is used in a wide variety of food products—such as ice cream, Cheez Whiz®, Nutri-Grain® bars, and many other substances. In ice cream, the sodium alginate prevents ice crystals from forming.

When poured into the calcium chloride solution, the sodium ions from the sodium alginate in the Gaviscon® trade places with the calcium ions. As a result, the polymer chains of the alginate become crosslinked, resulting in the formation of the polymer "worms." Crosslinking causes the polymer to become rigid. If the "worms" are allowed to remain in solution, they will become even more rigid.

The calcium ions are able to cause crosslinking because each calcium ion has a 2+ charge, which is able to bond to a 1– charge on two separate alginate polymer chains. The chemical name of the polymer worms is calcium alginate. The sodium ion, on the other hand, only has a 1+ charge, so it is not able to connect two separate alginate chains.

The Gaviscon® will form polymer "worms" in a drink that is fortified with calcium, but not in one that is not. The calcium ions will cause the alginate polymer chains in the Gaviscon® to crosslink and form polymer "worms." In the drink without calcium, no crosslinking occurs. This is an excellent test to see if a drink actually contains free calcium ions.

Interestingly, if Gaviscon® is added to milk, no polymer "worms" form. Even though milk contains a great deal of calcium, the calcium does not exist as free ions and is thus unable to cause crosslinking. Test other food substances with Gaviscon® to see if they too contain calcium ions.

Fun fact: There are nearly 2,700 species of earthworms in the world. Most are reddish in color, but there is a blue variety in the Phillipines and a green one in the United Kingdom. A typical acre of farmland may contain up to a million earthworms! The world's largest earthworm was found in South Africa, measuring 6.7 meters (22 feet) long.

Incredible Inedible Slime
Experiment Fifteen
MICROWAVEABLE SLIME!

The slime created in this experiment has excellent elasticity and durability. High temperatures are required to make this slime, however, so please exercise caution.

What you need
- Metamucil® (available in drug stores)
- Beaker or microwave-safe container
- Microwave oven
- Oven mitts
- Food coloring (optional)
- Popsicle stick for stirring

Safety precautions
Adult supervision required. This slime should not be tasted or eaten. Keep it away from young children and pets. The slime produced in this experiment will be very, very hot! Use potholders or insulated gloves when handling the beaker. Do not handle slime until after it cools.

How to make it
1. Place 5 mL (1 tsp) of Metamucil® in a large beaker or other microwave-safe container.
2. Add 240 mL (1 cup) of water, and stir. If desired, food coloring can be added.
3. Heat in the microwave for about 5 minutes, but keep a close watch on it. It will begin to boil and

then to rise. If it looks like it will spill out of the container, turn off the microwave and allow it to cool.

4. Repeat this process six times, each time heating the mixture until it begins to rise. Allow it to cool for five minutes between each heating. It will be very hot at this point, so exercise caution.

5. Allow to cool for an hour or so before touching.

What to do with it

1. When cool, remove the Metamucil® slime from the beaker. You have created your own microwaveable slime!

2. It can be bounced, pulled, stretched, and stepped on without losing its elasticity.

3. Store in a zip-lock bag. Keep in the refrigerator. If mold develops on the slime, discard it.

The science behind the slime

The microwaveable slime you created is an example of a gel, which is a colloidal suspension where a liquid is dispersed in a solid. Heating greatly facilitates the dispersion of the water into the Metamucil®. Metamucil® is a dietary supplement that helps to relieve constipation—primarily due to its high fiber content.

Fiber is composed of complex carbohydrates that differ from sugar and starch in that our bodies lack the necessary enzymes to digest them. But fiber is an important part of our diet because it aids in digestion and the removal of waste from the body. Metamucil® is 95% fiber.

There are two main types of fiber: water-soluble and water-insoluble. Sources of water-soluble fiber include foods such as oats, beans, peas, and certain types of fruits. Sources of water-insoluble fiber are bran, whole grains, and many vegetables.

Metamucil® is composed of psyllium husks, which are soluble in water. Psyllium husks comprise the outer coverings of seeds from certain varieties of the plantain plant, which is native to Iran and India. When these husks come into contact with water, they swell up, forming a gel. The formation of a gel is what makes Metamucil® so effective at relieving constipation, since it keeps the feces soft and moist. Here is an even more disgusting point to ponder: If your diet consisted solely of Metamucil®, your feces would resemble the slime that you just made in this experiment. Keep that in mind as you play with your slime!

It is the presence of mucilage (a type of fiber) in the psyllium husks that is primarily responsible for the absorption of water. In nature, this absorption of water by the seed husks aids in germination. Psyllium husks are 10–30% mucilage. Mucilage is also commonly used to make glue. Think of mucilage glue as a type of vegetarian glue, as opposed to gelatin-based glues, which are made from animal products.

Fun fact: To avoid constipation during his historic nine-day flight aboard the space shuttle Discovery in 1998, 77-year old astronaut John Glenn brought Metamucil® with him, as did 46-year old Japanese astronaut Chiaki Mukai. Glenn brought the apple crisp variety of Metamucil® wafers, while Mukai chose the cinnamon variety.

Incredible Inedible Slime
Experiment Sixteen
PLAY DOUGH SLIME!

The slime made in this experiment is similar in composition to the commercially available Play-Doh®. It can be molded into all sorts of interesting shapes, and unlike many other types of slime, it will tend to hold its shape.

What you need
- Flour
- Vegetable oil
- Cream of tartar
- Salt
- Food coloring
- Saucepan or beaker
- Large stirring spoon
- Heat source
- Zip-lock bag

Safety precautions
Perform only under adult supervision. Exercise caution when using stove. Wear safety goggles.

How to make it
1. Add 240 mL (1 cup) flour, 240 mL (1 cup) water, 5 mL (1 tsp) vegetable oil, 10 mL (2 tsp) cream of tartar, 60 mL (¼ cup) salt, and several drops of food coloring to a saucepan.

2. Stir thoroughly, until the mixture is free of all clumps.
3. Heat over medium heat for about 3 minutes or until the mixture begins to thicken. Remove from heat.
4. When cool, remove it from the pan. As you work it with your hands, it will develop a more pliable texture.
5. For an interesting variation, make Kool-Aid® play dough. Repeat the above procedure, except add a packet of unsweetened Kool-Aid® in place of the food coloring to give the play dough a unique color and scent.

What to do with it

1. Play dough can be molded into a variety of shapes. It holds its shape very well.
2. Play dough can be used to model virtually any scientific concept, from atoms to the solar system to parts of the cell.
3. Try placing an old penny in a hunk of play dough for a few days. How does the penny look after you remove it? Can you provide an explanation for this phenomenon?
4. Store the play dough in a zip-lock bag. If the play dough dries out, add water one drop at a time until it achieves the consistency you desire.

The science behind the slime

When heated, starch undergoes gelatinization (or thickening) in the presence of water. This is due to hydrogen bonding between the starch and water molecules. The granules of starch absorb water and swell up. This swelling begins when the temperature of the mixture reaches 60°C (140°F). The starch granules become a tangled, amorphous network at this point, losing all structure. This gives the play dough its unique texture. Play dough is actually an example of a gel. A gel is a colloid where a liquid is dispersed in a solid. Other examples of gels are jelly and gelatin.

The play dough is an effective penny cleaner because it contains cream of tartar, which contains tartaric acid. Many acids are highly effective at removing corrosion from metals, and thus are excellent copper cleaners and rust removers. Other acidic substances that are effective at cleaning pennies are vinegar, lemon juice, and carbonated beverages.

The cream of tartar is used in the play dough mixture to prevent crystallization of the salt particles. Acidic substances impede crystallization. If the salt were to form crystals during the making of the play dough, it would develop a grainy texture. The lack of crystallization helps to give the play dough a smooth texture.

Fun fact: The commercially available Play-Doh® was originally called Magic Wallpaper Cleaner, and was used to remove soot from walls stained by the burning of coal. Due to the diminishing use of coal for heating homes in the 1950s, this substance was renamed Play-Doh® and marketed to children as an easy-to-use modeling compound, since traditional modeling clay was too difficult for young children to work with. Play-Doh® originally came only in off-white. Colors were added in 1957.

Incredible Inedible Slime
Experiment Seventeen
GELATIN PLAY DOUGH SLIME!

Play dough is great fun to make. Adding gelatin makes for an interesting twist. Play dough slime made from gelatin has a slimier feel, and tends to hold its shape better than other types of play dough.

What you need

- Flour
- Salt
- Cream of tartar
- Vegetable oil
- Package of sugar-free fruit-flavored gelatin (9 g)
- Saucepan
- Measuring cups and spoons
- Stirring spoon
- Heat source
- Wax paper
- Zip-lock bag

Safety precautions

Adult supervision required. Exercise caution with boiling water. The mixture will be very hot—allow it to cool before handling. Wear safety goggles.

How to make it

1. Add 480 mL (2 cups) flour, 240 mL (1 cup) salt, 1 package of gelatin, and 60 mL (¼ cup) cream of tartar to a pan. Stir thoroughly.
2. Add 480 mL (2 cups) boiling water and 30 mL (2 tbsp) vegetable oil to the dry mixture in the pan. Stir thoroughly.
3. Heat the mixture over low heat on the stove until the mixture develops a uniform doughy consistency.
4. Remove the play dough from the pan with the spoon and allow it to cool on a piece of wax paper.

What to do with it

1. When the mixture is cool, remove the play dough slime from the wax paper with your fingers. Mold it into whatever shape you desire.
2. If you want your molded shape to become permanent, allow it to air dry for a few days. Otherwise, store it in a zip-lock bag to prevent it from drying out.

The science behind the slime

Gelatin is a protein, and is obtained by boiling animal bones and connective tissue containing collagen. Cow bones and pigskin are common raw materials used to make gelatin. Gelatin is colorless, odorless, and tasteless. In hot water it readily dissolves, and then forms a gel upon cooling. It is capable of absorbing up to ten times its own weight in water.

Gelatin is widely used in the food industry as a thickener and emulsifier, being found in yogurt, marshmallows, nougat, Gummi® bears, caramels, butter, ice cream, vitamin gel caps, jelly, sauces, and, of course, Jello®. It is also used in the making of glue, photographic film, detergents, fertilizers, pharmaceuticals, paper, and matches.

When used in making play dough, the gelatin helps to give it a unique texture. It works with the flour to absorb water and form a gel. Starch from flour will form a gel at a temperature from 60°–65°C, absorbing water and swelling up. As the starch-water mixture cools down, it becomes thicker or more viscous. The gelatin dissolves in hot water and gels when it cools back down (think of what happens when you make Jello®). As a result of this combination, a very interesting type of slime is formed.

Fun fact: Since 1956, more than 2 billion cans of Play-Doh® have been sold. This amounts to more than 700 million pounds! If formed into a snake, this much Play-Doh® would encircle the earth 300 times! By the way, September 16th is National Play-Doh Day.

Incredible Inedible Slime
Experiment Eighteen
CLAY SLIME!

The slime you will make here is just as slimy as any other type of slime, but with one big difference. It will eventually harden into a permanent piece of sculpture, which is distinctly non-slimy.

What you need
- Flour
- Salt
- Vegetable oil
- Food coloring
- Oven
- Measuring cups and spoons
- Large stirring spoon
- Bowl
- Cookie sheet

Safety precautions
Adult supervision required. Exercise caution when using oven. Do not touch the heated clay until it has cooled.

How to make it
1. Add 480 mL (2 cups) of flour, 240 mL (1 cup) of salt, 30 mL (2 tbsp) vegetable oil, and 240 mL (1 cup) of water to a large bowl.
2. Add several drops of food coloring until the desired color is achieved.

3. Mix thoroughly, until you have a uniform slimy consistency. If the mixture is too sticky, add a little more flour. If it is too dry, add a little more water a few drops at a time.
4. Remove the mixture from the bowl and knead it on the countertop until it is the consistency of bread dough.

What to do with it

1. Form the slime into whatever shape you desire. Do not make your sculptures too thin, or they will tend to crack when they dry out.
2. You can let your creations air dry for a few days, or dry them in the oven on a cookie sheet for about an hour at 120°C (250°F).
3. After heating, the clay will be hard as rock. Allow the hardened clay to cool before touching.
4. To make a non-hardening variety of clay, try this recipe: 240 mL (1 cup) flour, 60 mL (¼ cup) salt, 60 mL (¼ cup) vegetable oil, and 60 mL (¼ cup) water.

The science behind the slime

The recipe for this slime is very similar to that of the play dough slime made previously. However, there are several differences. Proportionally, there is less water in the clay recipe, so it hardens more quickly. If play dough is left exposed to the air, it will eventually dry out as well, but it takes much longer because of the fairly large water content that is bound up in the gel structure.

The clay slime also uses a much larger proportion of salt to flour. This larger concentration of salt will cause the slime to have a firmer texture, making it more conducive to clay formation.

You can buy clay that will never harden. These non-hardening varieties of clay are oil-based, and tend to resist drying out. The non-hardening version recommended above contains a larger concentration of vegetable oil than the hardening variety. Vegetable oil has such a large molecular weight that it evaporates very slowly.

Fun fact: The most basic form of clay is found in the soil. If this clay is heated in a special oven known as a kiln, it will harden. If straw is added to it, it sticks together much better, and is known as mud-brick or adobe. Humans first began using clay for building homes around 6000 BC.

Incredible Inedible Slime
Experiment Nineteen
SLIME IN A BOTTLE!

Unlike other varieties of slime you have made, this one will be contained within a bottle. It is still safe to touch, but is more fun if you keep it in a bottle and observe the fascinating swirling patterns that form.

What you need
- Liquid hand soap containing glycol stearate, not glycol distearate (some, but not all, brands of Softsoap® will work)
- 20 oz plastic soda bottle, or other suitable container
- Food coloring

Safety precautions
Do not taste or drink the slime in a bottle.

How to make it
1. Fill about one-fourth of the bottle with liquid soap.
2. Add no more than 5 drops of food coloring.
3. Slowly fill with water to avoid suds. Fill to the brim.
4. Screw cap on tightly and shake until well-mixed.

What to do with it
1. Invert the bottle to observe an interesting swirling pattern.

2. Roll the bottle on the floor or table and then suddenly stop it. What do you observe?
3. Obtain a tornado tube connector (available from a toy store) and connect an empty bottle of the same size to your bottle. Form a swirling tornado.

The science behind the slime

The interesting patterns that develop when your bottle is inverted are due to adding more soap than can be dissolved in the water. As a result, the water flows past these undissolved soap particles, creating interesting flow patterns. The food coloring makes these patterns more visible. This same effect is visible in commercially available "Flowmotion" tubes, which are made from similar materials.

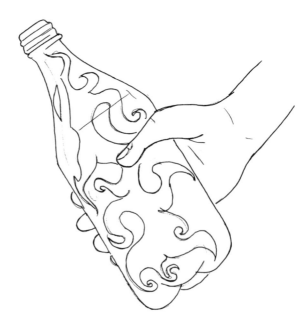

The slime in the bottle provides a good way to observe angular momentum, which refers to the tendency of rotating bodies to keep on rotating. When the bottle is rolled and suddenly stopped, the fluid within continues to move. The same thing occurs when you spin in circles and then stop. The fluid within the semicircular canals of your inner ear keeps moving, even though you have stopped. This continued movement of fluid gives you the sensation of motion, even though your body has stopped moving.

Fun fact: You can observe interesting swirls in a bottle of V-8 Splash® fruit drink. The color swirls are even mentioned on the label, where they are noted as a natural phenomenon. The swirls are produced by fruit juices that are not fully dissolved in the drink. As a result, the remaining liquid flows past this undissolved liquid, creating the swirling effect.

Incredible Inedible Slime
Experiment Twenty
FLUORESCENT SLIME!

Many objects fluoresce, or glow, under a black light. Slime can also be made to glow under a black light. In this experiment, you will make an incredibly awesome type of slime that will glow an otherworldly color when placed under a black light.

What you need
- Fluorescent highlighter
- Pliers
- Plastic cup
- Materials to make slime (from experiment one)
- Black light

Safety precautions
Adult supervision required. The fluorescent slime should not be tasted or eaten. Keep it away from young children and pets. Fluorescent substances are sometimes toxic. Wear safety goggles and wash hands when finished. Borax is toxic and irritating to the skin. **Do not stare at the black light—it emits ultraviolet light that is harmful to the eyes.**

How to make it
1. Using pliers, remove the fluorescent tip from a highlighter. Place it in a cup half- filled with water.
2. After 5 minutes, remove the tip from the water. The water will now be highly fluorescent.

3. Use the same recipe for slime that you used in experiment one, except use the fluorescent water in place of regular water in step 2.

What to do with it

1. Illuminate the slime under the black light in an otherwise darkened room. What do you observe?
2. Allow the slime to pass between your fingers as you view it under the black light.
3. Turn off the black light. Does the slime still glow?

The science behind the slime

The black light used in this experiment emits long wave ultraviolet (UV) energy. Although not as harmful as short wave UV light, which causes sunburns, care should be taken not to stare directly at the black light. Eye damage can result if you stare at the black light for prolonged periods of time, since its waves carry more energy than visible light.

UV light is invisible to humans; however, many insects can see UV light. Many commercially available "bug zappers" use UV light to attract insects. The violet light you see when a black light is turned on is actually visible light, which borders on the UV portion of the electromagnetic spectrum.

Fluorescent highlighters contain fluorescent pigments that can absorb UV light from a black light and immediately release this energy as visible light. When UV light is absorbed, electrons within these pigments become excited, immediately jumping up to a much higher energy level. As these excited electrons fall back to ground state, they emit visible light. This emission of visible light is what you see when fluorescent pigments glow under a black light. Fluorescence is defined as the property of absorbing UV light and then emitting visible light. By incorporating fluorescent pigments into your slime, it too can be made to fluoresce under the black light.

Try to discover other methods to make fluorescent slime. If you can find fluorescent glue or paint, try making slime with these substances.

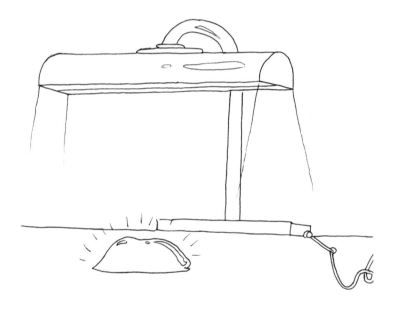

Fun fact: Scorpions will fluoresce brightly under certain wavelenths of ultraviolet light. If viewed under a black light, a pure black scorpion will glow bright green!

Incredible Inedible Slime
Experiment Twenty-one
GLOW-IN-THE-DARK SLIME!

Objects that glow in the dark are great fun. Slime that glows in the dark is even more fun. In this experiment, you will quickly and easily make slime that glows in the dark.

What you need

- Elmer's® white glue (or equivalent)
- 20 Mule Team Borax® (available in grocery stores)
- Food coloring
- 2-Liter bottle
- Eyedropper
- Popsicle stick for stirring
- Zip-lock storage or freezer bag
- Disposable plastic cups
- Glow-in-the dark paint or medium (available in hobby and craft stores; also available from Glow Inc. at 410-551-4874 or www.hobbyglow.com)
- Black light (optional)

Safety precautions

Adult supervision required. This slime should not be tasted or eaten. Keep it away from young children and pets. Borax is toxic and irritating to the skin and eyes. Wear safety goggles. **Do not stare at the black light—it emits ultraviolet light that is harmful to the eyes.**

How to make it

1. Follow the instructions for making slime in experiment one, except add some glow-in-the-dark paint or medium to the Elmer's glue. The amount added is not crucial.
2. After adding some glow-in-the-dark material to the glue in your cup, place the cup under a light bulb and proceed to a darkened room. If the glue does not glow brightly, add a little more of the glow-in-the-dark material.
3. Proceed with the making of your slime, following the instructions from experiment one.

What to do with it

1. Place the slime under an incandescent light bulb and then take the slime to a darkened room. How long does the slime glow in the dark?
2. Place the slime under a black light, if available. Then take the slime to a darkened room. Does it glow more brightly than when it was placed under an incandescent bulb?
3. Experiment with other light sources to "charge up" your slime, such as sunlight, a flashlight, or a fluorescent bulb. Then take the slime to a darkened room. How do the results compare with the other light sources?

The science behind the slime

The glow-in-the-dark compounds that you added to your slime are phosphorescent. Phosphorescent substances are also fluorescent, in that they glow brightly under a black light, but they differ in that phosphorescent compounds continue to glow after the light source has been removed. Like fluorescence, phosphorescence is due to the excitation of electrons. The electrons become excited and jump up to a higher energy level. As the electrons fall back to ground state, they emit the previously absorbed energy as visible light. The emitted light is often of a different wavelength than the absorbed light, such as when ultraviolet light is absorbed from a black light and emitted as visible light. However, the electrons stay excited for a longer period of time in phosphorescent compounds, gradually falling back to ground state. As the electrons gradually fall back to ground state, they emit light in the process. When all electrons have fallen back down to ground state, the object ceases to glow in the dark. In fluorescent compounds, electrons immediately fall back to ground state after excitation, which explains why these objects do not glow in the dark after the excitation source is removed.

Fun fact: Radium is one of the few chemical elements that glow in the dark. It was commonly used to make watch and clock hands glow in the dark, but its use for this purpose was eventually discontinued due to fears that the radioactivity emitted by radium could be hazardous to your health.

Incredible Inedible Slime
Experiment Twenty-two
FINGER PAINT SLIME!

Finger painting is not just for kids. It can be enjoyed by people of all ages who do not mind getting their fingers a little messy. The finger paint you will make in this experiment has a nice slimy texture that will make it a pleasure to work with. It is also completely nontoxic.

What you need
- Skim milk
- Beaker or microwave-safe container
- Food coloring
- Vinegar
- Eyedropper
- Coffee filter
- Plastic cups
- Film canister

Safety precautions
Adult supervision required. The finger paint slime should not be tasted or eaten. Exercise caution with boiling milk. Make sure milk is cool to the touch before handling.

How to make it
1. Place 60 mL (¼ cup) of skim milk in a beaker and heat in the microwave until the milk boils. This should take about 2–3 minutes.
2. Add 20 drops of food coloring. The mixture should be a very deep color.

3. Allow the milk to cool, then add vinegar with an eyedropper. This will cause the milk to curdle. Continue adding vinegar until no more curds form.
4. Pour this lumpy solution through a coffee filter that is supported over the drain in a sink. The liquid part should pass through the filter and the solids should remain. Discard the liquid and keep the solids, which will be contained within the coffee filter.
5. If the paint is too runny, allow it to air dry for a day or so until it becomes more viscous.

What to do with it

1. Store the paint in a film canister in the refrigerator until you are ready to use it for finger painting.
2. Add different colors of food coloring to make different colors of finger paint.

The science behind the slime

The primary protein found in milk is casein. Adding vinegar (acetic acid) will denature the casein proteins in milk, causing them to clump together to form curds. Denaturing involves changing a protein's chemical structure.

The denaturing of milk protein is pH dependent. Milk normally has a pH of about 6.5, and it will curdle at a pH of about 5.3. Milk will naturally curdle when it goes sour, due to the conversion of lactose (milk sugar) to lactic acid by bacterial action. Cottage cheese is primarily curdled milk. The first step in the manufacture of other types of cheese is to extract the curds, which are then subjected to further processing.

However, milk contains other proteins besides casein. Whey proteins are also present. Whey forms the clear liquid that you see on top of a container of yogurt or cottage cheese—just like in the nursery rhyme where little Miss Muffet sat on a tuffet eating her curds and whey. Whey proteins are not denatured by acids, but they are denatured by heating. This explains why the milk must first be heated.

All paints require a binder, which gives paint its thick consistency and provides adequate coverage when applied to a surface. The curds act as the binder and the food coloring acts as the pigment.

Fun fact: Cows cannot give milk until they have given birth to a calf. But even with continuous milking, cows will go dry after 10 months. When they give birth to another calf, they will resume giving milk.

Incredible Inedible Slime
Experiment Twenty-three
LATEX SLIME!

Latex is a naturally occurring form of rubber. In its liquid form, it is quite slimy, but it will make a very durable form of rubber if an acid is added to it. In this experiment, you will see the slimy latex instantaneously transform into a rubber ball.

What you need
- Liquid latex (used for making molds—available in craft and hobby shops)
- Disposable plastic cups
- Popsicle stick for stirring
- Vinegar

Safety precautions
Adult supervision required. The latex slime should not be tasted or eaten. Keep it away from young children and pets. Wear safety goggles. Do not do this experiment if you are allergic to latex. Only a very small percentage of the population (about 1–6%) is allergic to latex. Most allergic reactions are characterized by mild skin irritation similar to that caused by poison ivy. More severe symptoms may include nasal congestion, swelling around the mouth, nose, and throat, and difficulty breathing. If any of these symptoms occur upon exposure to latex, medical attention should be sought immediately. *(Author's note: I have used latex for many years with hundreds of children of all ages, and have yet to experience one case of even a mild latex allergy.)*

How to make it

1. Pour 30 mL (2 tbsp) of liquid latex into a disposable plastic cup.
2. Add 30 mL (2 tbsp) of water to the latex. Stir thoroughly.
3. Add 30 mL (2 tbsp) of vinegar to the latex solution. Stir vigorously and quickly. The latex will coagulate around your stirring stick.
4. Immediately remove the hardened latex from your stick and fashion it into a ball.
5. Rinse thoroughly with water and squeeze tightly to remove any excess latex. Make sure you keep your safety goggles on, as the latex can squirt out of the ball in all directions, making quite a mess.

What to do with it

1. Try bouncing your latex ball. If it is not perfectly round, will it bounce straight up into the air?
2. Over time, the latex rubber will cure and turn a darker brown and become more flexible. It is not necessary to keep your latex ball in an enclosed container. Experiment to see if your ball will rebound higher after the latex has cured for a few weeks.
3. Experiment to see what other shapes you can make from latex.

The science behind the slime

Liquid latex is obtained from the sap of rubber trees (*Hevea brasiliensis*) that grow in the Amazon rain forest. These trees are now widely cultivated in other tropical areas as well. The milky juice in a milkweed plant also contains latex.

Upon exposure to air, the latex sap from rubber trees will harden. If a rubber tree is damaged in the wild, this hardened latex will form a plug that will keep the tree from losing any more sap. (The same function is performed by the sap in a pine tree.) To prevent this hardening, ammonia is added to the latex after it is extracted from the tree. You may have detected the odor of ammonia in your liquid latex.

When vinegar is added to the latex, the ammonia is neutralized and the latex hardens. Since vinegar is a dilute solution of acetic acid, it will neutralize the aqueous ammonia, which is a basic solution. Neutralization reactions are very common, and occur when you take an antacid to relieve excess stomach acid. The products of a neutralization reaction are a neutral salt and water.

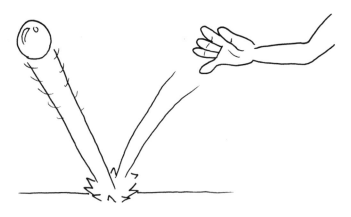

Latex is composed of long chains of C_5H_8 molecules, forming a polymer. In the liquid form these molecules are suspended in water in small globules (spherical structures). When the latex solidifies, these globules join together to form long chains that are randomly joined together in all directions. The elasticity of the latex ball you made is due to the fact that the polymer chains fold back on one another. It can be stretched out, but always returns to its original shape—sort of like an accordion.

Fun fact: Latex is used in over 40,000 different household items. Tires, balloons, rubber bands, gloves, and paint all contain latex.

Incredible Inedible Slime
Experiment Twenty-four
SUPER BALL SLIME!

The slime made in this experiment is a little different than other forms of slime. This slime actually bounces, sort of like a super ball. Yet, it is still slimy and moldable.

What you need

- Sodium silicate solution (available in hardware and drug stores, in the paint section)
- Ethyl alcohol (available in hardware and drug stores as denatured alcohol)
- Measuring cups
- Plastic sandwich bag
- Zip-lock bag

Safety precautions

Adult supervision required. The super ball slime should not be tasted or eaten. Keep it away from young children and pets. Sodium silicate is toxic if ingested, and is irritating to the skin and eyes. Wear safety goggles. Denatured alcohol is toxic if ingested, and is flammable. Read all safety instructions on the label of the container before using. Keep it away from open flames. Wash hands after handling the super ball slime.

How to make it

1. Add 20 mL (4 tsp) of sodium silicate solution and 10 mL (2 tsp) of ethyl alcohol to a sandwich bag. Seal the bag.

2. Tip the bag so the liquids accumulate in one corner, and mold them into a ball through the bag.
3. Remove the ball and rinse with water, continuing to shape it into a ball.

What to do with it

1. You may bounce the ball, but it will shatter if bounced too hard. If the ball shatters, squeeze the pieces together with your hand under running water.
2. Place the ball on a flat surface. Observe after a few minutes. What happens?
3. Store in a zip-lock bag.

The science behind the slime

The ethyl alcohol and sodium silicate bond together to form a silicone polymer, which has the properties of rubber. Crosslinking occurs between the silicate particles of the sodium silicate and the ethyl group $(- CH_2CH_3)$ of ethyl alcohol. As a result, long chains of the silicone polymer are formed, which have rubberlike properties. As a result, the ball you made will bounce. The ball appears to be a solid, but is actually a very viscous (slow-moving) liquid. It will slowly flow to assume the shape of its container. It will flatten out into a puddle if left on the table.

Fun fact: In January 1967, the American Football League (AFL) champion would play the National Football League (NFL) champion for the first time. This event was still unnamed when a member of the AFL came across his daughter's Superball™. He then suggested that the championship football game be called the Super Bowl. The rest is history.

Incredible Inedible Slime
Experiment Twenty-five
PLASTIC SLIME!

So many household items are made from plastic that it would be difficult to count them all. Many types of plastics get very soft upon heating. Small beads of these plastics, known as Friendly Plastic®, can be heated and then molded into various objects. In its liquid melted form, this plastic is very slimy and very moldable.

What you need
- Friendly Plastic® beads (Available from art supply stores; also available from Jewelry Supply at 916-780-9610 or www.jewelbay.com /EJS/ friendly plasticsindex.htm. A similar material known as Posmoulage can also be used. It is also available in art supply stores, or can be ordered from Dick Blick Art Materials at 800-723-2787 or www. dickblick.com.)
- Beaker or microwave-safe glass container
- Microwave oven or other heat source
- Wooden spoon
- Thermometer

Safety precautions
Adult supervision required. Wear safety goggles. Friendly Plastic® should not be tasted or eaten. Keep it away from young children and pets. Exercise caution with hot water. Do not touch Friendly Plastic® when it is hot. Handle with a spoon and allow it to cool a little before touching it with your hands.

How to make it

1. Fill a beaker about halfway with water and heat until the water is at least 70°C (158°F).
2. Add as many Friendly Plastic® beads as you would like to the hot water.
3. Allow the beads to remain in the water for a few minutes. They will turn from opaque to translucent and will form a single glob of plastic. Remove this glob with a wooden spoon.
4. Cool by running the plastic glob briefly under cold water, but not so much that it causes the plastic to harden.
5. The plastic should now be warm and moldable, but not so warm that it burns your fingers. If the plastic hardens before you have a chance to shape it, simply place it back into hot water for a few minutes.

What to do with it

1. While the plastic is still warm and moldable, fashion it into whatever shape you desire. Once it cools, it will harden.
2. If you made a ball, see if it will bounce.
3. If you want to make something else, reheat the plastic until it melts. You can then reform it into whatever you desire.
4. You can also purchase Friendly Plastic® in stick form from the website listed above, which also softens upon heating.

The science behind the slime

Friendly Plastic® is made of long chains of sodium polycaprilactone. It is an example of a thermoplastic polymer. A thermoplastic becomes soft upon heating. If you have ever left an object made of plastic on the dashboard of your car in the summertime and had it melt, you have already seen how thermoplastics are affected by heat.

As molecules are heated, they move farther apart, which leads to the translucent appearance of the beads as they are heated. Light passes through a translucent object, but not an opaque object. The molecules of the Friendly Plastic® spread out as they are heated, allowing light to pass through.

The Friendly Plastic® melts at a temperature of from 60–66°C (140–151°F). The polymer chains of which the friendly plastic is composed are long and unconnected, with little crosslinking between adjacent chains. This enables the plastic to be heated and reheated repeatedly. The melting of the Friendly Plastic® is a good example of a physical change, since no new chemical compound is created and the process is easily reversible.

Look for plastic items around your home with a recycling code of "4" on the bottom, which means they are composed of low density polyethylene (LDPE). LDPE is also a thermoplastic. Glue bottles, container lids, bags, and packing films are often made from this substance. Place these substances in boiling water to see if they will soften.

Fun fact: Friendly Plastic® is commonly used to make dental impressions of teeth. A patient bites down on a warm mass of soft plastic, which is then removed from the mouth. When the plastic hardens, it forms a permanent impression of the teeth.

Incredible Inedible Slime
Experiment Twenty-six
MUSTARD SLIME!

If you thought mustard was only for eating, think again. In this experiment, you will use mustard to make a truly unique type of slime. You will probably not want to touch it, but it is great fun to watch.

What you need
- Transparent plastic cup
- Mustard
- Baking soda (sodium bicarbonate)
- Ammonia
- Eyedropper
- Popsicle stick for stirring

Safety precautions
Adult supervision required. The mustard slime should not be tasted or eaten. Keep it away from young children and pets. Wear safety goggles when performing this experiment. Ammonia is irritating to the eyes and nose, and is toxic if ingested. Do not inhale ammonia fumes.

How to make it
1. Fill a disposable cup halfway with mustard.
2. Add about 15 mL (1 tbsp) of baking soda to the cup and stir briefly.
3. Cease stirring and observe.
4. Add more baking soda a little at a time, until the reaction ceases.

What to do with it

1. The incredible rising mustard makes a great chemical volcano.
2. Experiment with other types of condiments (such as ketchup) to see if the same effect occurs.
3. Add a few drops of ammonia to the rising mustard. What happens to its color?

The science behind the slime

The mustard will rise in a dramatic fashion due to the presence of vinegar in mustard. The reaction between the vinegar and baking soda will produce carbon dioxide gas, which causes the mustard to rise. Other condiments will produce the same effect if they contain vinegar. The reaction is as follows:

$$CH_3COOH_{(aq)} + NaHCO_{3(s)} \Rightarrow NaCH_3COO_{(aq)} + H_2O_{(l)} + CO_{2(g)}$$

    vinegar   baking soda   sodium acetate

Few people are aware that mustard is yellow due to an additive. If you read the ingredients on the label of a mustard container, it will list turmeric as an ingredient. Turmeric is derived from the root of a plant grown in the East Indies, and is used to dye mustard yellow. It is also an excellent base indicator, turning red in the presence of a base. Since ammonia is basic, mustard will therefore turn red when ammonia is added. (Baking soda is also basic, but its pH is not high enough to cause a color change in the turmeric.) If vinegar (which is an acid) is added, the ammonia is neutralized and the turmeric returns to its original yellow color.

Fun fact: France has played a prominent role in the history of mustard production, manufacturing favorites such as Grey Poupon®. However, French's® Mustard, which claims to be America's favorite, has nothing to do with France. It is named after the company's founder—Robert T. French.

Incredible Inedible Slime
Experiment Twenty-seven
BREAD SLIME!

No, you did not misread the title. You will actually make slime out of bread, which will be much slimier than you might think. It can be molded into all sorts of objects, and since this slime will eventually dry out and harden, your molded objects will become permanent.

What you need
- White bread
- Elmer's® glue
- Dish soap
- Bowl
- Spoon
- Measuring cups and spoons
- Zip-lock bag

Safety precautions
The bread slime made in this experiment should not be tasted or eaten.

How to make it
1. Remove the crust from seven pieces of white bread. Discard the crusts.
2. Break the bread into small pieces and add them to a bowl.
3. Add 35 mL (7 tsp) of Elmer's® glue.
4. Add 10 mL (2 tsp) of water.
5. Add 3 mL (approximately ½ tsp) of dish soap.

6. Stir thoroughly and then knead with your fingers until the substance obtains a thick, uniform consistency.
7. If the slime is too dry, add a little more water.

What to do with it

1. Use your hands to mold the bread slime into whatever shape you desire.
2. After about 24 hours, the slime should harden.
3. Store the bread slime in a zip-lock bag if you do not want it to harden right away.

The science behind the slime

Bread is made from flour, which is made from kernels of wheat. A wheat kernel has three main parts: the outer layer (bran), the embryo (wheat germ), and the endosperm (starch). During the milling of grain to make white flour, both the bran and the wheat germ are removed. This leaves the endosperm, the primary ingredient of white flour. About 70% of flour by weight is endosperm (or starch).

Starch is an excellent thickener, because granules of starch will readily absorb water and swell up when heated. The purpose of using white bread in this experiment is to obtain starch in a readily usable form. The dish soap acts as an emulsifier. An emulsifier acts to combine two substances that would otherwise not combine—in this case glue and starch. The resulting substance is known as an emulsion. As the water in the bread slime evaporates, it will dry out and harden—forming permanent sculptures.

Fun fact: The first loaf of sliced bread ever sold was in 1928 in Chillicothe, Missouri, as a result of the invention of a bread slicing machine by Otto Rohwedder. However, the sale of sliced bread was banned during Word War II by the Secretary of Agriculture—because the metal used to make bread-slicing machines was needed for the war effort.

Incredible Inedible Slime
Experiment Twenty-eight
SLIPPERY SLIME!

The slime you will make in this experiment is perhaps the slimiest of all the slimes. It is exceptionally shiny and slippery, which is all the more reason to make up a big batch today.

What you need

- Guar gum powder (available from a health food store or from CedarVale Natural Health, Inc. at 866-758-1012 or www.cedarvale.net/herbs/guar gumpowder.htm)
- Borax solution (see experiment one for instructions on how to prepare)
- 2-Liter bottle
- Food coloring
- Disposable plastic cups
- Popsicle stick for stirring
- Zip-lock bag
- Measuring cups and spoons
- Funnel
- Balloon
- Eyedropper

Safety precautions

Adult supervision required. This slime should not be tasted or eaten. Keep it away from young children and pets. Borax is toxic and irritating to the skin and eyes. Wear safety goggles.

How to make it

1. Prepare a solution of guar gum by adding 1 Liter of warm water to a 2-L bottle. Slowly add 10 mL (2 tsp) of guar gum powder. Shake vigorously for 10 minutes.

2. Pour some guar gum solution into a disposable cup. Add several drops of food coloring if desired.

3. Add the borax solution a few drops at a time with an eyedropper and stir. The slime will begin to form immediately. When most of the liquid has turned into slime, quit adding the borax solution. A good rule of thumb is to quit adding the borax when there is still a little liquid left on the bottom of the cup. This will ensure that you have not added too much borax. You will end up adding approximately 5 mL (1tsp) of borax solution for every 100 mL (20 tsp) of guar gum solution, if both solutions are saturated.

What to do with it

1. Remove the slime with your fingers. As you continue to work with the slime, it will become less sticky.

2. Using a funnel, add 250–500 mL (1–2 cups) of the slime to a bottle. Blow up a balloon part way and hold it closed while a friend helps you to slip it over the mouth of the bottle. Turn the bottle over to pour the slime into the inflated balloon. Be sure to hold the mouth of the balloon in place as you transfer the slime or you could end up with a big mess! Once the slime is all transferred into the balloon, carefully separate the balloon from the bottle, gradually let out the

excess air from the balloon, and then tie it off. You now have an excellent stress reliever.

3. Store the slime in a zip-lock bag in the refrigerator. If mold develops on the slime, discard it.

The science behind the slime

Guar gum powder is extracted from the seeds of the guar plant (*Cyamopsis tetragonoloba*). This plant is native to India. It is an example of a polysaccharide, with its molecules connected together in long linear chains to form a polymer. When mixed with water, these long chains weakly capture water and becoming entangled with one another. The resulting solution will be very viscous, making guar gum an excellent thickener and emulsifier in commercial food processing. It has about eight times the thickening power of cornstarch, and is widely used in dressings and sauces. It is also used in papermaking, cosmetics, and pharmaceuticals.

When the guar gum is added to the borax solution, crosslinking occurs between the borate ions contained within the borax solution and the guar gum polymer chains. A similar reaction occurs between the borax and Elmer's® glue (see experiment one). Think of the guar gum molecules as strands of spaghetti that easily slide past one another. The borax serves to hook together the strands of spaghetti at various points, preventing them from sliding past one another. The result is a tangled mass that produces a rubbery substance known as an elastomer—better known as slime.

Fun fact: The U.S. Marines once hired scientists to develop a type of slippery slime which could be sprayed to control crowds, break up riots, and help guard sensitive buildings such as embassies. The slime they developed has successfully stopped assailants both on foot and in automobiles. Its composition is top-secret, but the slime is made from material similar to soft contact lenses. It lasts from 6–12 hours, is environmentally friendly, and can be reactivated with water.

Incredible Inedible Slime
Experiment Twenty-nine
CHAMELEON SLIME!

Chameleons are tropical lizards that change color as a protective camouflage in response to their surroundings. In this experiment you will make slime that will change colors when you change its pH.

What you need

- PVA acid-free bookbinding glue (available in art supply stores or directly from the manufacturer, Books By Hand, at www.BooksByHand.com or 505-255-3534)
- Borax solution (see experiment one for instructions on how to prepare)
- Eyedropper
- Disposable plastic cups
- Zip-lock bag
- Popsicle stick for stirring
- Turmeric (available in grocery stores in the spice section)
- Washing soda (available in grocery stores in the laundry detergent section)
- Vinegar
- Ammonia

Safety precautions

Adult supervision required. This slime should not be tasted or eaten. Keep it away from young children and pets. Borax, washing soda, and ammonia are toxic and irritating to the skin and eyes. Do not inhale ammonia vapors. Do not allow any of these substances to contact your skin. Wear safety goggles.

How to make it

1. Follow instructions for making slime in experiment thirteen (Putty Slime), except this time add turmeric powder to the glue, but do not add food coloring. Add enough powder to make the glue a uniform yellow color. It is important that you stir very thoroughly in order to evenly distribute the powder within the glue. This slime is safe to touch.
2. Add a little washing soda to a cup and then add enough water to dissolve it. Stir thoroughly. Do not touch this solution.

What to do with it

1. Place the slime in a cup and add a little of the washing soda solution to the cup. What do you notice? Do not touch this slime.
2. Now add some vinegar to the same cup. What happens? Do not touch this slime.
3. Repeat this experiment with ammonia. Does a color change occur? Do not touch this slime.
4. Experiment with other household substances to determine if the slime will change color. Always read and follow instructions on the label of all substances before using them.

The science behind the slime

Turmeric gives mustard its yellow color (see experiment twenty-six) and is an excellent base indicator.

When a base is added, it turns red. Some varieties of goldenrod paper are also made with turmeric, causing them to turn red in the presence of a base as well. It is best to make the chameleon slime with pH-neutral PVA glue, since its neutral pH will not affect the color of the turmeric when added.

The chemical name for washing soda is sodium carbonate, which is a very basic substance. It has a pH of around 11. Borax is also basic, but its pH is not high enough to cause a color change in the turmeric. The higher the pH, the more basic the substance. Household ammonia also has a pH of around 11. Turmeric turns red at a pH of 8.6. A pH of 7 is neutral.

When vinegar is added, the color of the turmeric reverts back to yellow, since vinegar is an acid (acetic acid). Acids neutralize bases if added in sufficient quantities.

Fun fact: The flowers of some varieties of *Hydrangea* change color depending on the pH of the soil. Those grown in soil with a pH range of 5.0–5.5 will produce blue flowers, while those grown in soil with a pH range of 6.0–6.5 will produce pink flowers! This effect is due to the concentration of aluminum ions in the soil, which is highest in acidic soils and lowest where the soil is alkaline.

Incredible Inedible Slime
Experiment Thirty
GUM SLIME!

The slime produced in this experiment is made from gum arabic. Gum arabic has a thousand and one uses. One of those uses involves making slime. In this experiment you will make slime that has an unusual gummy texture. You will also discover a way to thicken your slime to whatever consistency you desire.

What you need
- Gum arabic (available from art supply stores in solution form; available in powder form from CedarVale Natural Health, Inc. at 866-758-1012 or www.cedarvale. net)
- Borax solution (see experiment one for instructions on how to prepare)
- Eyedropper
- Disposable plastic cups
- Popsicle stick for stirring
- Cornstarch

Safety precautions
Adult supervision required. This slime should not be tasted or eaten. Keep it away from young children and pets. Borax is toxic and irritating to the skin and eyes. Wear safety goggles.

How to make it

1. Pour some gum arabic solution into a disposable cup. Use whatever amount you desire.
2. Stirring constantly, add borax solution a few drops at a time until it forms a gel.
3. Continue to stir vigorously for several minutes.

What to do with it

1. Pour half of the slime into a separate cup.
2. Add a little cornstarch to the slime until it thickens up. Be careful not to add too much, or the slime will become too thick and will fall apart.
3. Compare the viscosity of the slime without the cornstarch to that of the slime with the cornstarch.

The science behind the slime

Gum arabic is obtained from the stems and branches of acacia trees, which grow in Africa in the sub-Saharan region. It is produced naturally by these trees in large nodules as a way to seal up wounds in the bark of the tree, through a process known as gummosis.

Gum arabic is a complex polysaccharide (many sugar units linked together), and thus is used extensively as a thickener and emulsifier. It is also used in food, textiles, paint, ink, cosmetics, and pharmaceuticals. Gum arabic is found in art supply stores because of its use in watercolor painting. It increases the brilliance, gloss, and transparency of watercolors.

In the powder form, gum arabic is very soluble. As its concentration in water increases, it becomes more viscous. Adding borax links together the polymer chains of the gum arabic molecules, causing them to acquire a thick, slimy texture. A gel is formed as water becomes suspended within the polymer matrix. Adding cornstarch makes the slime even more viscous, since cornstarch is an excellent thickener.

Fun fact: Gum arabic is widely used in a variety of food products. The next time you eat JuJuBes®, gum drops, or cough drops, look on the label to see if the product contains gum arabic.

Incredible Inedible Slime
Experiment Thirty-one
JEL SLIME!

The slime you will make in this experiment utilizes a commercially available substance known as Clear Jel®. Clear Jel® is made from modified food starch and is commercially used as a food thickener. When mixed with hot water, it makes an excellent slimy gel, which will provide you with hours of slimy fun.

What you need
- Clear Gel® food thickener (Available from restaurant supply stores or food specialty stores. It can also be purchased online at http://www. bluechipgroup.net/ products/instantclearjel. htm or 801-263-6667)
- Blender
- Beaker or microwave-safe container
- Tablespoon
- Microwave oven or other heat source
- Zip-lock bag

Safety precautions
Adult supervision required. Wear safety goggles. Exercise caution with hot water.

How to make it
1. Heat about 240 mL (1 cup) of water in a beaker to boiling.

2. Pour this water into a blender. Turn on the blender to medium speed.
3. Slowly add about 30 mL (2 tbsp) of the Clear Jel® to the water in the blender.
4. Blend until all clumps have disappeared, and you have a clear slimy gel.
5. Allow to cool before handling.

What to do with it

1. The gel that forms is a fascinating substance to play with, and can be molded and shaped into a variety of different forms.
2. Color the gel with food coloring. Try mixing different colors of gel to create new colors.
3. Store the gel in a zip-lock bag.

The science behind the slime

Clear Jel® is made from modified food starch. It is an example of a polymer with many molecules of starch ($C_6H_{10}O_5$) linked together to form clusters. Clear Jel® has been pre-gelatinized (pre-cooked), enabling it to gel instantly without cooking. It is an excellent thickener, and is often used as a substitute for cornstarch, flour, or tapioca. Clear Jel® is commonly used in bakeries and also for frozen food. It is superior to other thickeners because it is clear in color when cooked, is very stable, and remains smooth. It also prevents liquids from separating and curdling after foods have been frozen. Several varieties of Clear Jel® are available—some varieties are used in foods that require cooking, and others are used in uncooked foods. Either variety will work well for this experiment.

Fun fact: Clear Jel® is pure carbohydrate. All carbohydrates furnish 4 Calories (C) of energy per gram. Protein also furnishes 4 C per gram—while fat furnishes a whopping 9 C per gram. What we commonly refer to as Calories are actually kilocalories. Calories written with a capital "C" are actually kilocalories, while calories written with a small "c" are true calories. There are 1000 calories (small c) in 1 Calorie (large C). Thus that apple you ate this morning actually contained 80,000 calories—not 80!

Incredible Inedible Slime
Experiment Thirty-two
PECTIN SLIME!

If you have ever made jelly, you have probably used pectin. Pectin is used to give jelly its gel-like consistency. But pectin can also be used to make some very cool slime, as you will shortly see.

What you need
- Large beaker or microwave-safe glass container
- Package (49 g) of powdered pectin (available in grocery stores or department stores—in the canning supplies section)
- Microwave oven or other heat source
- Denatured alcohol (available in hardware or drug stores)
- Popsicle stick for stirring
- Zip-lock storage bag
- Eyedropper

Safety precautions
Adult supervision required. This slime should not be tasted or eaten. Keep it away from young children and pets. Exercise caution when heating water and the resulting mixture—it will be very hot! Denatured alcohol is toxic and flammable. Keep it away from flames. Wear safety goggles.

How to make it

1. Heat about 240 mL (1 cup) of water to boiling. Handle the hot beaker with a potholder.

2. Add powdered pectin a little at a time, stirring vigorously. Be careful not to allow any clumps to develop.

3. When no more pectin readily dissolves, heat the mixture in the beaker to boiling again. Be careful not to allow the mixture to boil for too long, or it will overflow. Handle the beaker using a potholder.

4. Repeat steps 2 and 3 until the entire package of pectin has been dissolved. It should produce a thick, viscous solution. Allow the mixture to cool. (If you cannot dissolve the entire package of pectin, that is all right—just try to dissolve as much as possible.)

5. Once the mixture has cooled, add denatured alcohol a few drops at a time until a thick ball of slime forms around the stick. Rinse thoroughly with water before touching. Once all the alcohol has been removed, use your fingers to remove a huge ball of slime!

What to do with it

1. Once you have removed the slime with your fingers, examine its properties. Is it a solid or a liquid? Can it be stretched? Does it bounce? What effect does cooling have on the slime?

2. Store the slime in a zip-lock bag when finished playing with it. If mold develops on the slime, discard it.

The science behind the slime

Pectin is a naturally occurring complex carbohydrate. Fruits such as apples, plums, grapes and cranberries contain a great deal of pectin, especially in the skins and cores of the plant. The cell walls of plants contain pectin, which help to give the plant its rigid structure. Plants soften upon heating due partly to the dissolving of the pectin in the cell walls of the plant. When fruit ripens, pectin is also lost. Commercially available powdered pectin is made by extracting pectin from the peels and cores of apples or other fruits rich in pectin.

Pectin is most commonly used as a gelling agent in jellies and jams, but can also be found in yogurt, baby food, and candies. Since pectin is a polymer, it is composed of long chains of molecules. Each of these chains has a negative charge, which causes them to repel one another. Acids reduce this electrical charge, allowing pectin molecules to gel more readily. Commercially available pectin usually contains added acid; the natural acid found in fruits also helps gelling. However, acids alone are not sufficient to cause pectin to gel. In an aqueous solution, pectin molecules are more likely to bond with water than with each other. The addition of sugar alleviates this tendency by dehydrating the solution, causing the pectin molecules to bond with each other, forming a gel. Most commercially available varieties of pectin contain some added sugar in the form of dextrose (glucose).

In the experiment you performed, the ethyl alcohol took the place of the sugar. The water molecules in the pectin solution have a greater affinity for the alcohol than they do for the pectin. In other words, water would rather bond with alcohol than pectin. As a result, pectin will precipitate out as a solid. All of the water does not bond with the alcohol, however. Some water molecules remain weakly bonded to the pectin molecules, and the suspension of these pectin molecules in water forms a gel. This gel makes up our pectin slime.

Fun fact: Kaopectate®, an anti-diarrhea medicine, derives its name from the fact that it originally contained kaolin (clay) and pectin. Pectin is an excellent intestinal regulator, and is very effective at counteracting diarrhea.

Incredible Inedible Slime
Experiment Thirty-three
PAPER SLIME!

You might not think there is much of a relationship between paper and slime. But if you visit a paper mill you will see quite a bit of slime being generated. This slime is known as pulp. In this experiment, you will not make paper from scratch, but will instead recycle newspaper. In doing so, you will discover that paper-making is indeed a very slimy business.

What you need
- Newspaper
- Cornstarch
- Measuring cups and spoons
- Blender
- Window screen mounted on a frame (a screen used to put over aquariums works very well; you can also make your own by nailing some screening material over a frame made with boards)
- Ruler
- Jar or beaker

Safety precautions
Exercise caution when using blender. Trying to blend a mixture of water and too much paper may burn out the blender—use only the recommended amount.

How to make it

1. Tear up a double-size sheet of newspaper into tiny pieces and place in a beaker or jar.
2. Add 240 mL (1 cup) of water.
3. Add 10 mL (2 tsp) of cornstarch.
4. Stir for 10 minutes or until the paper has turned into pulp.
5. Place in a blender and blend for 1 minute. The mixture should be totally liquefied. If not, blend for another minute or so.
6. Pour the liquefied pulp back into the beaker.
7. Place the screen over the sink or in a place where it can drain. Pour the pulp over the screen. Using your ruler, straighten the edges and smooth out the pulp until it becomes a thin layer.

What to do with it

1. After several days, remove the piece of recycled paper. Make sure it is totally dry before you remove it.
2. Write on your recycled paper with a marker. How is it similar to real paper? How is it different?
3. Make colored paper by adding food coloring to the pulp and then repeating the above procedure.
4. Experiment with other types of paper besides newspaper. How do these types of recycled paper compare with recycled newspaper?

The science behind the slime

Paper is made by first cutting wood into tiny pieces. The wood is then chemically treated to remove the lignin, leaving nearly pure cellulose. Lignin is a hard material found in the cell walls of plants, which helps to give the plant support but which must be removed from wood before it can be made into paper. Cotton or linen fibers are also added during the paper-making process. The pulp is then bleached, spread on screens, drained, pressed, and dried.

The waste products that result from making paper take a heavy toll on the environment. If you have ever driven by a paper mill, you probably noticed a foul odor. So recycling paper is definitely good for the environment.

In the experiment you performed, the cornstarch makes an excellent thickener and binds together the cellulose fibers used to make recycled paper. The slimy mixture you created will eventually make paper once the water evaporates. Your paper will probably be more like cardboard, with a grayish appearance from the ink. To make white paper you would have to chemically bleach the material. If you wanted thinner paper, the recycled material would need to be pressed.

Fun fact: The term pulp fiction refers to works of sensational writing involving love and crime that were printed on cheap paper. They reached their heyday in the 1930s and 1940s. The paper used to print this type of fiction was nearly all wood pulp. The cheaper the paper, the higher the concentration of pulp.

Incredible Inedible Slime
Experiment Thirty-four
APPLESAUCE SLIME!

Applesauce and cinnamon taste great together. They also make a great type of slime. Since this is the one of the easiest types of slime to make, give it a try. You will be amazed at the result!

What you need
- Applesauce
- Cinnamon
- Bowl
- Measuring cups and spoons
- Zip-lock bag

Safety precautions
Do not taste or eat the applesauce slime.

How to make it
1. Add equal amounts of applesauce and cinnamon, by volume, in a bowl. 15 mL (1 tbsp) of each is a good amount to start with.
2. Mix thoroughly until a brown, slimy ball of uniform consistency is formed.

What to do with it
1. The slime can be molded into whatever shape you desire. After a few days, it will harden if exposed to the air.

2. To keep the slime from drying out, store in a zip-lock bag in the refrigerator.

The science behind the slime

The difference between applesauce and apple juice is that applesauce contains pectin, among other things. Pectin is a constituent of the cell wall in plants and helps to give fruit its firm texture. It is added to jams and jellies to help thicken them. In the experiment you performed, the pectin in the applesauce acts to thicken the slime and thus gives it its unique texture.

Cinnamon is obtained from the bark of trees of the laurel family found in Southeast Asia and has been used as a spice since ancient times. Its aromatic qualities are due to cinnamon oil, a volatile compound found within the cinnamon. Cinnamon is used in everything from candy to medicine to soap. In the slime you made, cinnamon helps to absorb the water in the applesauce, acting as a binder to hold the ingredients together.

As the water within the applesauce slime evaporates, it becomes hard. It will smell very aromatic for quite some time, since the volatile oil within the cinnamon evaporates slowly.

Fun fact: Most "cinnamon" that is sold in the United States is actually a related spice known as cassia. True cinnamon is tan-colored, while cassia is a dark reddish-brown color.

Incredible Inedible Slime
Experiment Thirty-five
FROG EGG SLIME!

There is nothing quite as slimy as a mass of frog's eggs. The slime you will make next looks so much like frog's eggs that you will be expecting tadpoles to hatch from it at any moment!

What you need
- Plain tapioca
- Microwave oven or other heat source
- Beaker or microwave-safe container
- Measuring cups and spoons
- Potholder
- Zip-lock bag

Safety precautions
Adult supervision required. Exercise caution when boiling water. Do not touch slime until it cools.

How to make it
1. Add 240 mL (1 cup) of water to a beaker.
2. Heat the water to boiling.
3. Add 45 mL (3 tbsp) of tapioca to the water. Stir thoroughly.
4. Heat the mixture to boiling.
5. Allow the mixture to cool.

What to do with it

1. When the slime has sufficiently cooled, remove it from the beaker with your fingers.
2. Rinse with water to remove the stickiness. As you continue to work with the slime, it will become less sticky. It will look similar to frog eggs.
3. To make colored frog's eggs, add some food coloring to the water before you add the tapioca.
4. Vary the amount of tapioca added to see how this affects the consistency of your frog egg slime.
5. Store in a zip-lock bag in the refrigerator. If mold develops on the slime, discard it.

The science behind the slime

Tapioca is a type of root starch, which is derived from the roots of a tropical plant known as either cassava or manioc. Root starches differ from other starches in that they have little taste and are composed of much longer chains of molecules. These long chains make tapioca an excellent thickener. When you buy tapioca in the store, it comes in the form of little hard pellets. They are manufactured this way to prevent long stringy masses of the long polymer chains from forming.

Tapioca is primarily used to make pudding, but it also makes excellent slime. When heated, the hard tapioca pellets soften and form a gel by absorbing water. A gel forms anytime a solid is suspended in a liquid. Gels are examples of colloids. In colloids, true dissolving does not occur, but rather one substance is suspended in another.

Fun fact: A single mass of bullfrog eggs can measure 60 centimeters (about 2 feet) in diameter and contain up to 20,000 eggs. Predators, however, consume most of the eggs and only a few ever hatch into tadpoles. Leeches are especially fond of frog eggs.

Incredible Inedible Slime
Experiment Thirty-six
SILICONE SLIME

The commercially available Silly Putty® is made from a silicone compound. In this experiment, you will make slime that is also made from silicone. Your slime will be similar to Silly Putty®, not only in feel, but also in chemical composition.

What you need
- White 100% silicone rubber sealant (available in hardware stores)
- 20 Mule Team Borax®
- Talcum powder (baby powder)
- Mineral oil (available in drug stores)
- Moisturizing body lotion
- Measuring cups and spoons
- Disposable plastic cups and spoons
- Popsicle stick for stirring

Safety precautions
Adult supervision required. This slime should not be tasted or eaten. Keep it away from young children and pets. Wear safety goggles. Read the label on the container of silicone rubber sealant before proceeding. The sealant is an eye and skin irritant, and is toxic if ingested or inhaled. Use only in a well-ventilated area and do not allow the substance to contact your skin. Borax is also toxic and is an eye and skin irritant. Mineral oil is toxic if ingested.

How to make it

1. When measuring out the silicone, use only disposable cups and spoons. Measure out 10 mL (2 tsp) of silicone rubber sealant and place in a cup. Do not touch it and do not inhale the vapors.
2. Add 10 mL (2 tsp) of mineral oil. Stir thoroughly.
3. Add 5 mL (1 tsp) of borax powder. Stir thoroughly until completely mixed.
4. Add 2.5 mL (½ tsp) of talcum powder. Stir thoroughly.
5. Add 5 mL (1 tsp) of moisturizing lotion. Stir thoroughly.
6. Scoop out the mixture with a spoon and rinse thoroughly with water. It is now safe to touch. If it still feels sticky, allow it to sit for about a half-hour. If it still feels grainy, some undissolved borax is probably still in the slime. Rinse thoroughly with water until the graininess disappears.

What to do with it

1. Mold the slime into a rubber ball while it is still pliable. It will become more firm with time.
2. Attempt to bounce it. After a couple of days, bounce it again. What do you notice?
3. Attempt to pull it apart. How is it similar to Silly Putty? How is it different?
4. After a couple of days, attempt to pull it apart. What do you notice?

The science behind the slime

Silicone compounds are inorganic polymers, composed of long chains of alternating silicon and oxygen atoms that form the backbone of these molecules. By contrast, organic polymers are carbon-based. Attached to each silicon atom within this chain are two groups of different atoms. The specific properties of a particular silicone compound depend on the identity of the groups of atoms attached to the silicon atoms. Another name for a silicone polymer is polysiloxane.

Since the backbone chain contained within silicone compounds is very flexible, the compounds have a variety of applications. Silicones make excellent elastomers, which is just a fancy name for any material that has elastic properties, such as rubber. Caulking compound, breast implants, and Silly Putty® are all examples of silicone compounds that are elastomers. You can also find silicones in cleaning solvents, hand cream, cosmetics, cleanser, hair and skin care products, antiperspirants and deodorants, paint, lubricating oils, medicine, and detergents.

The slime you made in this experiment results from the crosslinking of the silicone polymer chains by the borate ions within the borax solution. This linking makes the material much more viscous. Volatile compounds within the silicone also evaporate, eventually making the slime much more firm. The commercially available Silly Putty® is also made from silicone compounds. It is made by reacting silicone oil with boric acid, which are similar to the compounds you used. Silly Putty® is known as a dilatant, meaning it acts like a solid when pressure is applied quickly but acts more like a liquid when pressure is applied slowly.

Fun fact: Over two million containers of Silly Putty® are sold in the United States each year.

Incredible Inedible Slime
Experiment Thirty-seven
ARROWROOT SLIME!

The type of slime made here is smooth, slippery, and very easy to make. It is one of the most beautiful slimes you can make, with a shimmering shine that will surely make this one of your favorites.

What you need
- Arrowroot powder (available in health food stores or from CedarVale Natural Health, Inc. at 866-758-1012 or www.cedarvale.net)
- Beaker or microwave-safe container
- Food coloring
- Measuring cups and spoons
- Microwave oven or other heat source
- Zip-lock bag

Safety precautions
Exercise caution when using boiling water. Wear safety goggles. Do not touch slime until it cools. If mold develops on the slime, discard it.

How to make it
1. Add 240 mL (1 cup) of water to a beaker. Add several drops of food coloring if desired.
2. Heat the water until it boils.
3. Add 60 mL (4 tbsp) of arrowroot powder to the boiling water. Stir thoroughly.
4. Heat the mixture to boiling.

What to do with it

1. When the slime has cooled, pull it out with your fingers.
2. Make another batch of slime but adjust the recipe by using less powder. How does this affect the consistency of the slime?
3. Adjust the recipe again by using more powder. How does this affect the consistency of the slime?
4. Store it in a zip-lock bag in the refrigerator. If mold develops on the slime, discard it.

The science behind the slime

Arrowroot is obtained from the root of the *Maranta* plant, which grows in the West Indies. Arrowroot is an example of a root starch, and is composed of very long amylose chains. An amylose chain is a polymer made up of repeating units of amylose, which is a type of starch. As a result of these long polymer chains, arrowroot makes an excellent thickener. It will form a gel at lower temperatures than cornstarch, and less is needed to achieve the same thickening power. It is one of the easiest starches to digest, and has little taste.

When water is added to arrowroot powder, the starch granules swell up and undergo the process of gelatinization. Unlike other types of starch, arrowroot will form a gel even in cold water. However, it will form a gel more easily in hot water.

Fun fact: In addition to its use as a thickener, arrowroot has also been used as a bath and body powder and to draw poison from insect and snake bites.

Incredible Inedible Slime
Experiment Thirty-eight
TOOTHPASTE SLIME!

Who said toothpaste can only be used for brushing your teeth? You can actually use toothpaste to make a really nice type of slime that is both bouncy and stretchy. Just don't try to brush your teeth with this slime!

What you need
- Toothpaste (regular paste, not gel)
- Elmer's® white glue
- Cornstarch
- Disposable plastic cups
- Popsicle stick for stirring
- Measuring cups and spoons
- Zip-lock bag

Safety precautions
Adult supervision required. This slime should not be tasted or eaten. Keep it away from young children and pets. Toothpaste is harmful if ingested.

How to make it
1. Add 5 mL (1 tsp) of toothpaste, 10 mL (2 tsp) of glue, 20 mL (4 tsp) of cornstarch, and 5 mL (1 tsp) of water to a cup. Stir thoroughly.
2. If the mixture is too sticky, add a little more cornstarch. If the mixture is too crumbly, add a little more water. But only add very small amounts until the desired consistency is achieved. Even a

slight excess of water will make the slime very sticky.

3. Is the slime dries out, add water one drop at a time and work it in with your hands until the desired consistency is achieved.

What to do with it

1. Observe the elastic properties of this slime by stretching it slowly and then quickly.

2. Roll the slime in a ball and attempt to bounce it. Does the slime bounce?

3. Toothpaste contains abrasives that help to clean our teeth. Can you devise an experiment to test for these abrasive substances?

4. Make a fresh batch of toothpaste slime, except substitute a gel toothpaste for the paste toothpaste. Does slime still form? Do research to determine how gel toothpaste differs from paste toothpaste.

5. Store the slime in a zip-lock bag.

The science behind the slime

The first toothpaste was made by the ancient Egyptians around 3000 BC. It was composed of pumice, myrrh, burned egg shells, water, and the ashes of oxen hooves. We have come a long way since then! Today's toothpaste is a bit more sophisticated, plus it tastes better. The active ingredient is fluoride, which helps to prevent tooth decay. In this experiment, however, we are interested in the inactive ingredients. Toothpaste also contains abrasives such as calcium carbonate (chalk) or silica (sand).

The foaming that you get when you brush your teeth is due to detergents added to the toothpaste, usually sodium lauryl sulfate. Humectants—such as glycerin and sorbitol— help to give toothpaste its texture and also help it to retain moisture. Thickeners make the toothpaste very viscous. Common thickeners are carrageenan, cellulose gum, and xanthan gum. It is these thickeners that are the vital ingredient in the toothpaste slime, helping it to become a viscous blob that is so much fun to play with.

The cornstarch also acts as a thickener, effectively absorbing water and helping to bind the ingredients together. The Elmer's® glue contains polyvinyl acetate, which is a polymer. This substance helps to give the slime its elastic properties.

Fun fact: Collectively, Americans brush their teeth 200 billion times per year, and spend 1.6 billion dollars per year on toothpaste!

Incredible Inedible Slime
Experiment Thirty-nine
FROZEN SLIME!

The slime obtained from this experiment is for those who are too lazy to make their own. High quality slime can be inexpensively obtained from commercially available soft freezer packs. You will also observe how freezing affects the properties of this slime.

What you need
- Soft, reusable freezer pack (commercially available under various trade names—available in department, grocery, and sporting goods stores)
- Freezer
- Scissors
- Zip-lock bag

Safety precautions
Adult supervision required. This slime should not be tasted or eaten. Keep it away from young children and pets. Even though the slime obtained from the freezer packs is considered non-toxic, appropriate precautions should be taken.

How to make it
1. Cut open the freezer pack with a pair of scissors.
2. Remove the slime!

What to do with it

1. Put the slime in a zip-lock bag and place it in the freezer overnight. What observations can you make?

2. Remove the slime from the freezer and record how long it takes for the slime to thaw.

3. Place the same amount of water in a separate zip-lock bag and place it in the freezer. After it freezes, remove the bag from the freezer and record how long it takes for the ice to melt. How does it compare with the slime? What are the advantages in using slime in freezer packs to keep foods cool as opposed to using just plain water?

4. Store the slime in a zip-lock bag.

The science behind the slime

Freezer packs come in a variety of shapes, sizes, and formulations. The type of slime found within each will vary. The clear or whitish varieties of slime within the freezer packs tend to have a nicer consistency. Some of the blue slimes, such as Rubbermaid's Blue Ice®, tend to be somewhat grainy. Experiment with a variety of different types of freezer packs to determine which contains the best slime.

Most of the slime found within freezer packs is probably made from polyvinyl alcohol (see experiment ten). You will also notice plenty of empty space within the freezer pack. After freezing, the pack will be much tighter. This shows that the slime contains a great deal of water, since water is one of the few substances that expands when it freezes.

The water suspended within the gel matrix will not leak out even if the bag develops a small hole. The slime also enables the pack to be easily wrapped around objects that you wish to keep cold, such as aluminum cans. Increased surface contact means better heat transfer from the can to the gel, which decreases the time it takes to cool down the contents of the can.

Fun fact: The first electric refrigerator with a separate freezer compartment was introduced in the 1920s. To produce cooling, toxic gases such as ammonia, methyl chloride, and sulfur dioxide were used. Unfortunately, several fatalities occurred when these gases leaked out, leading to the widespread use of a much safer gas known as Freon. Freon has now been discontinued in the U.S. due to evidence that it may be harmful to the ozone layer.

Incredible Inedible Slime
Experiment Forty
CHEWING GUM SLIME!

Even though the average American chews nearly 200 pieces of gum per year, few ever stop to think about all of the cool science that goes into every single piece. In this experiment, we will learn all about the properties of this amazing substance.

What you need
- Pack of sugarless gum
- Cup
- Hot water
- Stirring spoon
- Freezer

Safety precautions
Keep chewing gum slime away from pets and small children—it may pose a choking hazard.

How to make it
1. Remove the wrappers from an entire pack of sugarless gum.
2. Place the gum in a cup of very hot tap water.
3. After about 5 minutes, or when the gum has considerably softened, remove it with a spoon.

What to do with it

1. Test the chewing gum slime for elasticity. When you stretch it, does it snap back to its original position?
2. Roll the chewing gum slime into a huge ball. Attempt to bounce it. What happens?
3. Place the chewing gum slime in the freezer for a few hours. Now attempt to bounce it. What happens?
4. Mold the chewing gum slime into various shapes and let it harden.
5. Repeat the above procedure with different brands of sugarless gum. Do you notice any differences?
6. Repeat the above procedure with gum that contains sugar. Do you notice any differences?

The science behind the slime

Chewing gum has been around for thousands of years. The first gum was made from the semi-hardened resin of evergreen trees. American pioneers added beeswax to make resin more chewy. The first commercially available chewing gum was sold in 1848 and was known as the State of Maine Pure Spruce Gum. The first bubble gum was invented by Frank Fleer in 1906, and was originally named Blibber-Blubber.

Up until World War II, chewing gum was made from chicle, a form of natural rubber that was obtained from the latex sap of the Central American sapodilla tree. (Chicle is the source of the brand name Chiclets®, a popular brand of chewing gum.) Chicle is a polymer composed of many repeating units (monomers) of isoprene (C_5H_8).

During World War II, there was much experimentation to produce artificial types of rubber, since natural rubber supplies were not adequate to keep up with demand. Out of these efforts arose synthetic rubbers that are now primarily used to make the gum base in chewing gum. These synthetic rubbers may be composed of substances such as styrene butadiene, polyvinyl acetate, or polyethylene. These synthetic rubbers have many of the same properties as chicle. They soften in the mouth and become very brittle when cooled to below 0°C.

When gum is manufactured, these natural and synthetic gum bases are melted down to form a thick syrup. Sugar, corn syrup, and softeners are then added, making the mixture more viscous. After this, flavorings and colors are added. The gum is then cooled, kneaded, and formed into the appropriate shape.

When gum is placed in hot water, the sweeteners and flavorings dissolve, leaving primarily the rubber that makes up the gum base. This rubber has some interesting properties. It has very little elasticity when warmed, meaning it does not snap back to its original shape when stretched. This lack of elasticity is responsible for the fact that it does not bounce at all. In order to bounce, a substance must have at least some elasticity. When placed in the freezer the rubber hardens, giving it a little bit of elasticity and thus a slight bounce.

Gum has been used for many things besides chewing. Since gum makes a good temporary adhesive, it can be used to seal leaks in gas tanks and garden hoses. The chewing of gum during air travel can open the Eustachian tubes (the tubes leading from your middle ear to your throat), thus helping to equalize differences in air pressure on the inside and outside of your eardrum. A liquid gum base can serve as an effective insecticide. Insects attracted to it get their jaws stuck together and starve to death. Spearmint gum can also repel household pests in your kitchen cupboards.

The downside to gum chewing are the wads that are surreptitiously stuck nearly everywhere, especially the undersides of theater seats, chairs, and tables. The best way to remove gum from carpets and upholstery is to freeze it, which makes it brittle and easy to remove. Commercial gum remover sprays make the gum extremely cold and brittle. The New York Central Railroad once had a full-time employee whose sole job was to remove gum from Grand Central Station. He averaged about seven pounds of gum per night, with double this amount on the weekends!

Fun Fact: The world's largest bubble, as recognized by the Guinness Book of World Records, was blown by Susan Montgomery Williams in 1994. It had a diameter of 58 centimeters (23 inches)!

Part II
INCREDIBLE
EDIBLE SLIME

All slime produced in this portion of the book may be eaten. All glassware, chemicals, and materials used in the inedible slime section of this book should be kept separate from the materials and equipment used to make edible slime. All edible slime should be made in the kitchen, not in a science laboratory. The slime produced here should be stored in the refrigerator, and eaten within a day or so after making. And remember—play with your food before eating it!

Incredible Edible Slime
Experiment One
TAFFY SLIME!

In this experiment, you will make a type of slime commonly known as saltwater taffy, which is not only very tasty but also incredibly slimy.

What you need
- Table sugar
- Light corn syrup
- Salt
- Butter
- Oil of peppermint
- Food coloring
- Saucepan
- Cookie sheet
- Stove
- Wooden spoon
- Candy thermometer
- Scissors
- Wax paper

Safety precautions
Adult supervision required. Exercise caution when heating the solution—it will be very hot! Do not handle until it is cool to the touch.

How to make it

1. Add 480 mL (2 cups) sugar, 240 mL (1 cup) corn syrup, 8 mL (1½ tsp) salt, and 240 mL (1 cup) water to a saucepan.
2. Cook slowly and stir constantly until the sugar dissolves.
3. After the sugar dissolves, cease stirring. Heat to 129°C (265°F) and then remove from heat.
4. Add 30 mL (2 tbsp) butter and 7 drops of food coloring. Stir thoroughly.
5. Pour the contents onto a buttered cookie sheet.
6. Allow the mixture to cool until it is comfortable to the touch. Then add 1 mL (¼ tsp) oil of peppermint. Stir thoroughly.

What to do with it

1. After buttering your hands, form the taffy into a ball and pull. Continue pulling on the taffy until it becomes difficult to pull. This will take anywhere from 10 to 20 minutes.
2. When the taffy gets lighter in color and becomes difficult to pull, cut it into small pieces with a pair of buttered scissors. Make each piece about a centimeter thick and about 2 centimeters long.
3. Wrap each piece of taffy in wax paper.
4. Enjoy your edible slime (also known as salt water taffy).
5. When making taffy again, experiment with other flavorings besides oil of peppermint.

The science behind the slime

Cooking is chemistry—plain and simple! Anytime you cook, you are performing chemical reactions. Since reactions generally speed up at higher temperatures, heating is often necessary for reactions to occur.

Many of the ingredients in this recipe—like sugar, salt, and oil of peppermint—give the taffy its flavor. Other ingredients serve to give the taffy its unique texture, which can also affect its flavor. The corn syrup and butter, for example, serve as interfering agents. Corn syrup is composed of long chains of glucose molecules that prevent the sucrose (table sugar) molecules from crystallizing. Crystallization of the sugar would make the taffy coarse and grainy. The proteins in the butter also interfere with crystal formation. The prevention of sugar crystallization also explains why you stop stirring after the sugar dissolves. Stirring or other types of mechanical agitation can cause sugar molecules to crystallize, which is the bane of candy making.

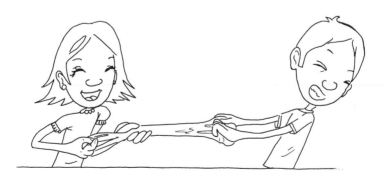

A crucial aspect of taffy-making is to pull it back and forth in long strands repeatedly. When taffy is made commercially, a machine is employed that does the strenuous work of pulling the taffy back and forth. The constant pulling of the taffy serves to aerate it. Aeration introduces many tiny air bubbles into the candy mixture, giving it a light and fluffy texture.

Fun fact: Do you know where the name "salt-water taffy" originated? Nobody knows for sure, but rumor has it that a shopkeeper in Atlantic City in 1883 had his merchandise flooded by a summer storm. The taffy was saturated with saltwater, and thus the name "saltwater taffy" was born.

Incredible Edible Slime
Experiment Two
PUDDING SLIME!

Everyone loves pudding. But have you ever stopped to think about how this delightfully slimy substance is made? In this experiment, you will make your own pudding from scratch, and learn all about the chemistry involved in making it.

What you need
- Nonfat dry milk
- Sugar
- Cornstarch
- Butter
- Vanilla extract
- Yellow food coloring
- Saucepan
- Measuring cups and spoons
- Stirring spoon
- Heat source
- Bowls

Safety precautions
Adult supervision required. Exercise caution when using stove and when pouring hot liquids.

How to make it
1. Add the following ingredients to a saucepan: 140 mL (28 tsp) nonfat dry milk, 70 mL (14 tsp) sugar, 55 mL (11 tsp) cornstarch, and 1 mL (¼ tsp) salt.

2. Slowly add 480 mL (2 cups) water. Stir until the contents are thoroughly mixed.
3. Stirring constantly, heat over medium heat until the mixture comes to a boil.
4. Turn the heat down to low and allow the mixture to boil gently for 3 minutes. Continue to stir.
5. Remove from heat. Add 30 mL (2 tbsp) butter, 5 mL (1 tsp) vanilla extract, and several drops of yellow food coloring. Stir until the butter has completely melted.
6. Allow to stand for about 15 minutes. Then stir again and pour into a serving bowl.

What to do with it

1. Refrigerate the pudding slime. When it has cooled, enjoy it. What does cooling do to the viscosity of the substance? Do you know what causes the "skin" to form on pudding?
2. Predict what would happen if any of the above ingredients were left out.
3. Formulate a recipe to make a different flavor of pudding, such as chocolate. Would the flavor affect your choice of food coloring?

The science behind the slime

If you read the ingredients on a box of commercial pudding, you will notice many of the same ingredients that are found in the above recipe. Depending on the brand of pudding, xanthan gum and carrageenan—polysaccharides that are very effective thickeners—may also be included.

The most important ingredient in pudding is starch. Heat turns the starch to gelatin because the starch granules swell up and absorb water, producing the viscous mixture we commonly know as pudding.

The skin that often appears on pudding is due to evaporation of water from the starch, resulting in a hardening of the surface. The formation of this skin can be prevented by placing a layer of plastic wrap directly on top of the surface of the pudding while it is cooling, so that the surface water does not evaporate. The skin does not appear on instant pudding, which does not require heating. As a result, the evaporation of water from its surface occurs very slowly.

Fun fact: September 19th is National Butterscotch Pudding Day.

Incredible Edible Slime
Experiment Three
PEANUT BUTTER PLAY DOUGH SLIME!

This variety of edible slime is quick and easy to make. Not only does it feel great when you are kneading it in your hands, but it tastes great. It is also one of the more nutritious varieties of edible slime.

What you need
- Creamy peanut butter
- Honey
- Nonfat dry milk
- Bowl
- Measuring cups and spoons
- Zip-lock bag

Safety precautions
None (unless food allergies exist)

How to make it
1. Add 2 parts (by volume) peanut butter, 1 part honey, and 4 parts dry milk to a bowl. (For a single serving, begin with about 15 mL (1 tbsp) of peanut butter. For larger groups, begin with a cup of peanut butter.)
2. Mix all ingredients thoroughly with a spoon or your fingers until it develops a uniform doughy consistency.

What to do with it

1. Once the desired consistency has been achieved, you can shape and mold your edible slime into a variety of shapes.
2. When you tire of playing with your slime, eat it!
3. Store the remainder in a zip-lock bag.

The science behind the slime

Honey is the stored food of the honeybee, primarily *Apis mellifera*. The honeybee is not native to North America, but was introduced by European settlers around 1625. Honeybees collect the nectar of flowers and store it in their crops as they carry it back to a hive. Enzymes modify the nectar and produce the sugars of honey. In the hive, the bees store the honey in cells and, by fanning the hive with their wings, reduce its moisture content, thereby producing viscous honey.

Different types of flowers produce honey of distinct flavors. Some types of flowers, such as certain species of rhododendrons and azaleas, produce nectar that will result in honey that is toxic to humans. Fortunately, this rarely occurs in North America. Up to 80% of honey is pure sugar, primarily fructose and glucose.

The peanut is not native to North America either. It is native to South America, and was eventually introduced to the United States by way of Portuguese explorers. Technically, the peanut is not a nut, but rather a seed. Before World War II, it was primarily used for livestock feed. Today, half of all peanuts used in the U.S. go toward the making of peanut butter.

Nonfat dry milk is made by evaporating nearly all of the water from skim milk. Without water, spoilage is not a problem, since bacteria cannot grow in it. The absence of fat also prolongs the shelf life.

When honey, dry milk, and peanut butter are mixed, the result is a tasty treat with a nice doughy consistency. The honey serves as a binder that holds the other ingredients together.

Fun fact: If a single honeybee were to produce a pound of honey, it would require the equivalent distance of three orbits around the earth to gather enough nectar! In actuality, a single honeybee gathers enough nectar to produce only a fraction of an ounce of honey during its lifetime.

Incredible Edible Slime
Experiment Four
GELATIN SLIME!

Gelatin (such as Jello®) has been a staple in American households for generations. Hospitals and schools seem particularly enamored by this slimy substance. However, you can do many other things with gelatin besides eating it!

What you need
- Two packages of gelatin dessert (one colored red and the other colored blue)
- Pan
- Stove
- Stirring spoon
- Cake pan
- Measuring cups and spoons
- Laser pointer

Safety precautions
Adult supervision required. Exercise caution when boiling water. Never look directly at a laser or point it at another person's eyes. Permanent eye damage may result.

How to make it
1. Add a package of gelatin (85 g) to 150 mL (10 tbsp) of boiling water in a bowl. Stir until the gelatin has completely dissolved. Pour into a cake pan and refrigerate. After the gelatin has set, cut it into cubes.

2. Use the method described above to make both red and blue gelatin.

What to do with it

1. Cut out a cube of red gelatin from the pan and shine a red laser through it. What do you observe?
2. Cut out a cube of blue gelatin and shine a red laser through it. What do you observe?
3. When finished with these observations, eat your gelatin cubes.

The science behind the slime

Gelatin is an example of a colloid, an evenly dispersed mixture that scatters light due to its large particle size. Specifically, gelatin is a gel, which is a colloid composed of a solid dispersed in water. The gelatin prepared in this experiment is firmer than ordinary gelatin, since it is made with less water.

When you shine a laser through the red gelatin, the laser beam is clearly visible within the gelatin itself. The tiny particles of red gelatin reflect the red light of the laser, making it visible. It is for this reason that the red gelatin transmits red light.

However, because the blue pigment within the gelatin absorbs red light, the laser is not visible in blue gelatin, nor does it come out the other side! Blue gelatin absorbs the other colors of light and reflects only blue light. Therefore, the red laser beam is not visible, since the red light is absorbed and is actually turned into heat.

Laser beams are very visible if shone through white fog, because white reflects all wavelengths of light. The only way our eyes can perceive a color is if that color is reflected toward our retinas. Certain pigments reflect certain wavelengths of light and absorb others. The wavelengths that are reflected are what our eyes perceive as color.

Lasers come in other colors besides red. What do you think would happen if a blue laser were shone through blue gelatin? What if it were shone through red gelatin? Instead of using a laser, light emitting diodes (LEDs) of different colors can be used. They can be purchased very inexpensively from Radio Shack and can easily be hooked up to a battery. You can then clearly see, for example, what happens when a blue light is shone through blue gelatin. When using LEDs, make sure you match the voltage of the LED to the voltage of the battery you are using.

When you shine your red laser through the other colors of gelatin, what happens? Does the laser beam pass through? Is it absorbed? The results may surprise you. Read the ingredients on the packages to gain some insight.

Fun fact: Forensic scientists duplicate human body parts from gelatin to test the effect of gunshot wounds on human victims. This ballistic gelatin is denser than normal gelatin, since it is formulated to be at the same density as human tissue.

Incredible Edible Slime
Experiment Five
GUMMY BEAR SLIME!

Gummy bears are fun to eat and even more fun to make. You will make your own version of gummy bears that are remarkably similar in texture to the types you can buy in the store.

What you need
- Flavored gelatin dessert with sugar
- Unflavored gelatin
- Food coloring
- Stove or other heat source
- Pan
- Stirring spoon
- Beaker or measuring cup with spout
- Candy molds or bottle caps from plastic soda bottles
- Store-bought Gummi® Bears
- Distilled water
- Salt water

Safety precautions
Adult supervision required. Exercise caution with stove and when using hot water. Do not touch the gummy bears until they have sufficiently cooled. Since gummy bears may pose a choking hazard, keep them out of the reach of young children.

How to make it

1. Add a box (85 grams) of flavored gelatin dessert and 50 grams (about 7 packets) of unflavored gelatin in a beaker.
2. Add 120 mL (½ cup) of boiling water to the beaker. Stir thoroughly.
3. Add food coloring, if desired.
4. Stir thoroughly until the powder has dissolved.
5. Pour the liquid into candy making molds or bottle caps.

What to do with it

1. When the mixture has cooled, remove it from the mold. Your gummy bear is now ready to eat.
2. When the mixture has hardened in the beaker, remove it. It will look like a flexible sheet of rubber. This too is edible.
3. Experiment with different flavors to give your gummy bears a different taste. Try adding lemon juice, Karo® syrup, honey, or other concentrated sugar additives to your mixture.
4. Place a gummy bear in distilled water overnight. What happens?
5. Place a gummy bear in salt water overnight. What happens?
6. Repeat steps 4 and 5 above with store-bought Gummi® Bears. Compare the results with your gummy bears.

The science behind the slime

Gummy bears are primarily made from a concentrated solution of gelatin, making them very chewy and elastic. In hot water, gelatin dissolves, forming a gel when it cools down. The commercially available Gummi® Bears have additional flavorings and colorings, along with additives to produce specific aromas. Bee's wax is added to give them their shine and also to prevent them from sticking together. Gelatin is produced from animal bones and connective tissue, but for Gummi® Bears only tissue from pigs is used.

When placed in distilled water, your gummy bear should have expanded considerably. The store-bought Gummi® Bears can expand up to six times their volume in distilled water. Results will vary with the homemade version of your gummy bears. They expand because water will always diffuse from a region of high water concentration to a region of low water concentration. The concentration of water is lower within the gummy bear than without, so water will diffuse into the gummy bear, expanding its size.

In salt water, the gummy bear will shrink considerably. Water will diffuse out of the gummy bear, because the concentration of water is initially greater within the gummy bear than in the saltwater solution. Diffusion will continue to occur until equilibrium is achieved, which occurs when the concentration of water is equal both within and outside of a substance.

The gummy bears act similar to the commercially available Gro-Beast® polymers, which come in the shape of various animals or dinosaurs. They can expand to over 30 times their original volume due to the ability of water to diffuse from high to low concentrations.

Fun fact: Gummi® Bears originated in Germany, and they derive their name from the fact that *Gummi* is the German word for rubber.

Incredible Edible Slime
Experiment Six
A SLIME MILKSHAKE!

Everyone loves a milkshake. This quick and easy slime milkshake is not only healthier than a typical milkshake, but is also quite delicious!

What you need
- Milk
- Tall glass
- Food grade guar gum (available from a health food store or from CedarVale Natural Health, Inc. at 866-758-1012 or www.cedarvale.net/herbs/guar gumpowder.htm)
- Chocolate syrup
- Sugar
- Measuring cups and spoons

Safety precautions
None

How to make it
1. Pour about 120 mL (4 fl oz) of milk into a tall glass. Add 5 mL (1 tsp) of chocolate syrup and 15 mL (1 tbsp) of sugar. Stir thoroughly.
2. Add 15 mL (1 tbsp) of guar gum powder and stir vigorously until the mixture thickens to your desired consistency.

What to do with it

1. You can drink your shake right away, or put it in the freezer, let it thicken, and eat it later with a spoon.
2. For a thinner shake, repeat the above procedure with less guar gum. For a thicker shake, add more guar gum. You can make the shake as thick as you would like if you add enough guar gum.
3. For a vanilla shake, omit the chocolate syrup and add a dash of vanilla extract instead.
4. Repeat the above experiment with skim, 2%, and whole milk. Is there a difference in the thickness of the milkshakes formed?

The science behind the slime

Guar gum powder is an example of a polysaccharide, with its molecules connected together in long linear chains to form a polymer. It is an excellent food thickener. Look for it on the labels of various food products. When mixed with the water in milk, these long polymer chains capture water and becoming entangled with one another. The resulting solution is a thick, viscous milkshake.

Does the idea of using guar gum to make a milkshake sound disgusting to you? Then consider the ingredients used to make milkshakes from three popular fast food restaurants.

First of all, here is a list of ingredients used to make McDonald's® vanilla milkshake mix:

- whole milk
- sucrose
- cream
- nonfat milk solids
- corn syrup solids

- mono- and diglycerides
- guar gum
- imitation vanilla flavor
- carrageenan
- cellulose gum
- vitamin A palmitate

Here is a list of ingredients used to make a Burger King® vanilla milkshake:

- milkfat and nonfat milk
- sugar
- sweet whey
- high fructose corn syrup
- corn syrup
- natural and artificial vanilla flavor
- guar gum
- mono- and diglycerides
- cellulose gum
- sodium phosphate
- carrageenan
- natural flavors from plant sources

Finally, here are the ingredients for a Wendy's® Frosty, which is thicker than a typical milkshake:

- milk
- sugar
- cream
- corn syrup
- whey
- nonfat milk
- cocoa
- dextrose
- guar gum
- mono- and diglycerides
- carrageenan
- calcium sulfate

- disodium phosphate
- vitamin A palmitate
- artificial and natural flavors

A quick glance at each list will reveal that all of the milkshakes have guar gum (among other ingredients) in common. Guar gum is very commonly used in the food industry as a thickener. The thickness you enjoy in a milkshake is no accident—it is due to the addition of guar gum.

Another substance that appears on all three lists is carrageenan. Carrageenan is an example of a polysaccharide, which is composed of long chains of galactose sugar molecules. It is a seaweed extract, and is commonly used in the food industry. Carageenan is an excellent thickener. It also acts as an emulsifier, helping to keep the proteins within the milk from separating out and coagulating. In addition, carageenan prevents the formation of ice crystals, which helps to gives the milkshake its creamy texture. In the food industry, this is known as enhancing "mouthfeel." So the next time you enjoy that delicious milkshake, remember that it is only possible because of guar gum and seaweed!

Fun fact: The straws in McDonald's® restaurants are deliberately designed to be wider in circumference than the straws used at other fast food restaurants. The wider straws make it easier to drink their viscous, guar gum-enriched milkshakes!

Incredible Edible Slime
Experiment Seven
BUTTER SLIME!

Making butter is much easier than you may think. In this experiment, you will not only make butter, but also make whipped cream and buttermilk. And all this comes from only one substance—cow's milk!

What you need
- Heavy whipping cream
- Clear glass baby food jar (or equivalent)
- Sugar
- Salt

Safety precautions
None

How to make it
1. Fill a baby food jar about a third of the way with heavy whipping cream. Make sure you tightly fasten the lid.
2. Shake the jar vigorously with a rapid up-and-down motion.
3. After each minute of shaking, open the jar and taste the contents. Observe how the whipping cream has changed in texture and appearance. Continue to shake the jar for several minutes.

What to do with it

1. After a minute or so of shaking, whipped cream will form. If you want to eat the whipped cream, remove some and add a little sugar.
2. After shaking for a few more minutes, butter will form. This too can be eaten. Before eating the butter, rinse several times with cold water to remove the buttermilk. Also, press excess liquid from the butter to prevent it from souring too quickly. You also may want to add a little salt to the butter to improve its taste.
3. The liquid left over from butter-making is buttermilk. You can drink the buttermilk, but it tastes really sour! It can also be used for cooking.

The science behind the slime

Heavy whipping cream contains 36–40% butterfat. It naturally rises to the top in milk because cream is less dense than the watery portion of the milk. When milk is homogenized, the fat droplets are broken up into tiny pieces, which remain suspended in the milk. Cream must be obtained from unhomogenized milk, and can be skimmed off the top. Skim milk is what remains after the cream is removed. Cream is an example of an emulsion, since it is composed of fat particles which are suspended in water. Proteins within the milk, known as casein, act as an emulsifying agent, preventing the fat and water particles from separating after the milk is homogenized.

When the cream is agitated, it becomes more viscous, eventually forming whipped cream. This cream is an example of a colloidal foam, since air is suspended within the mixture. The introduction of air is responsible for the increase in volume as the whipped cream forms.

Cream is an example of a rheopectic substance, because its viscosity is affected by agitation. As the cream is continually agitated, its viscosity increases, producing whipped cream. Cream is an example of a non-Newtonian fluid, since factors other than temperature affect its viscosity.

Continued agitation of the cream will eventually cause the fat molecules to form together into a semisolid mass known as butter. Agitation breaks up the original emulsion of fat and water, causing the fat molecules to coalesce into larger granules. In pioneer times, butter was made by constantly churning the cream in a butter churn. Butter is known as a reverse emulsion, since it consists primarily of solids with water molecules suspended within the fat. Butter contains about 80% milk fat, 18% water, and 2% milk solids such as protein and salts.

The liquid that is left over from butter-making is appropriately known as buttermilk. Due to its low pH of 4.0–4.8, it has a distinctly sour taste. Regular milk is only slightly acidic, having a pH of 6.4–6.8.

Fun fact: In the days before refrigeration, salt was added to butter as a preservative. Salt is still added to butter today, but primarily as a flavoring.

Incredible Edible Slime
Experiment Eight
OOZING GREEN SLIME!

The slime made in this experiment is fun to make and even more fun to eat. It has a slimy consistency that is somewhat of a cross between Jello® and pudding. It has a sweet, milky taste that kids seem to enjoy more than adults.

What you need
- 396 g (14 oz) sweetened condensed milk
- Cornstarch
- Green food coloring
- Stove or other heat source
- Saucepan
- Stirring spoon
- Thermometer
- Measuring cups and spoons

Safety precautions
Adult supervision is required. Exercise caution when using stove. Do not eat the slime until it has thoroughly cooled.

How to make it
1. Empty the can of sweetened condensed milk into a saucepan.
2. Add 15 mL (1 tbsp) of cornstarch and stir thoroughly.

3. Cook over low heat and stir constantly. You will need to heat for several minutes. The mixture must be heated to at least 60°C (140°F).
4. When the slime thickens to the consistency of gravy, remove the pan from the heat.
5. Add about 15–20 drops of green food coloring. Stir thoroughly.
6. Pour into a bowl and place into the refrigerator. How does this affect its viscosity? How does this affect its taste?

What to do with it
1. When the slime has cooled, it may be eaten.
2. Freeze the slime. How does this affect its taste? How does this affect its viscosity?
3. Make the slime with different colors. Does the color of the slime affect its perceived taste?
4. Experiment with the above recipe. Add more cornstarch. How does this affect its thickness? What can you do to change its taste?

The science behind the slime

Sweetened condensed milk is milk with about half of its water removed. This is accomplished by placing the milk in a vacuum, not by heating it. A vacuum is a region of greatly reduced air pressure. A perfect vacuum would contain no air and thus no air pressure. By reducing the atmospheric pressure above a liquid, the water molecules are free to evaporate at a more rapid pace.

To make sweeetened condensed milk, 20 grams of sugar are added for every 100 grams of condensed milk. This high sugar content produces an environment that is not conducive to the growth of microbes, enabling canned milk to be stored unrefrigerated indefinitely without spoiling. Since the concentration of dissolved solutes is greater outside of the microbe than on the inside, water will diffuse outward by osmosis through the cell membrane of the microbe in an attempt to equalize the concentrations. As a result, the microbe is dehydrated and killed. The solution surrounding the microbe is hypertonic, meaning it has a higher solute concentration than the solution within the microbe. Adding salt will preserve foods in the same way.

When cornstarch is added to the above mixture and it is then heated, the slime will begin to thicken. Cornstarch is an excellent thickener. Interestingly, starch granules absorb little water until they reach a temperature of around 60°C (140°F). At this point, the starch granules swell up considerably, creating a viscous solution with water. It is believed that at temperatures lower than this, the intermolecular bonds between individual starch molecules are so strong that little water can be absorbed. But once the ideal temperature of 60°C is reached, these bonds are broken, and the starch granules absorb water and swell up. This process is known as gelatinization, since a gel is formed between the starch and water. A gel is an example of a colloid, where a solid is permanently suspended within a liquid.

Fun fact: When making slime of any variety, green is the most commonly used color among children. Blue is the second most commonly used color, followed by red and then yellow.

Incredible Edible Slime
Experiment Nine
CARAMEL SLIME!

Caramels are delightfully slimy, especially when they are being made. The chewy texture of caramels is due to some fascinating changes that occur in the composition of sugar as it is heated. We will explore these changes in the following experiment, as well as make some very tasty caramel candy in the process.

What you need
- Sugar
- Heavy whipping cream
- Light corn syrup
- Salt
- Butter
- Vanilla extract
- Saucepan
- Heat source
- Wooden stirring spoon
- Measuring cups and spoons
- Candy thermometer
- Square baking pan (about 10 in x 10 in)

Safety precautions
Adult supervision required. Exercise caution when using stove and when heating liquids. The solution produced in this experiment will be very hot! Be careful when pouring the mixture. Do not eat until the mixture has thoroughly cooled.

How to make it

1. Thoroughly butter the sides and bottom of the square baking pan and then place aside.
2. Add 240 mL (1 cup) of sugar, 240 mL (1 cup) of heavy whipping cream, 120 mL (½ cup) of corn syrup, and about 1 mL (¼ tsp) of salt to the saucepan. Stir thoroughly.
3. Heat over low heat and stir constantly. As soon as the sugar has dissolved, add 60 mL (4 tbsp) of butter. Stir constantly.
4. Attach the candy thermometer to the side of the pan. Make sure the bulb of the thermometer is immersed in the solution, but not touching the bottom of the pan.
5. Once the mixture comes to a boil, as evidenced by bubbling, cease stirring.
6. Heat until the mixture reaches 120°C (248°F). Remove from the heat.
7. Add 2.5 mL (½ tsp) of vanilla and stir thoroughly.
8. Pour into the buttered pan.

What to do with it

1. When the caramel slime has cooled, cut it into squares and eat it.
2. Test for the plasticity of your caramel slime by seeing how far you can stretch it before it breaks.
3. Refrigerate the slime and then attempt to stretch it. Does cooling make it more or less plastic?

The science behind the slime

Candy making consists of heating a concentrated sugar solution until it forms the desired properties you are seeking. The longer the solution heats, the more concentrated it becomes as more water is boiled off. Firmer candies, such as peanut brittle, are made by heating a sugar solution to a high temperature. Higher temperatures result in a lower water concentration. Softer candies, such as fudge, are made by heating a sugar solution to a lower temperature. Lower temperatures result in a higher water concentration.

The temperature at which the caramel solution boils will be higher than the normal boiling point of 100°C, because dissolved solutes always create a boiling point elevation. As water boils away, the solution becomes more concentrated. As this solution cools, it may become supersaturated, which means it will contain more dissolved solute than it is supposed to have at that temperature. When a supersaturated solution is agitated or cooled too quickly, the excess solute can crystallize out. This can be good or bad, depending on the type of candy you are making. If you hope to make rock candy, this crystallization is necessary.

Caramel slime forms due to a chemical reaction between the sugar and the milk proteins in the cream. This reaction is known as the Maillard reaction, named after the French scientist who discovered it. The Maillard reaction is very common in cooking, and is responsible for the brown color of bread crusts, chocolate, coffee beans, dark beers, and roasted nuts and meats. When you roast marshmallows or make meringue, the browning is due to the Maillard reaction. The brown color of your caramel slime is also due to the Maillard reaction.

This reaction occurs when a sugar molecule reacts with the amine (nitrogen- containing) group of an amino acid. Amino acids are the structural units that make up all proteins. So you must have a sugar and a protein in order for the Maillard reaction to occur. The Maillard reaction is highly complex, with hundreds of intermediate by-products often formed. Its exact mechanism is not completely understood, but we can still take advantage of its benefits.

The corn syrup is composed of long chains of glucose molecules that prevent the sucrose molecules in table sugar from crystallizing. The corn syrup is known as an interfering agent, since it prevents the crystallization of sucrose. If the sucrose molecules crystallized, the caramels would have a grainy texture. The milk proteins in cream and butter also act as interfering agents, preventing sucrose formation and contributing to the creamy texture of the caramels.

In the above recipe, it is important to cease stirring once the solution has come to a boil. This is an additional measure to prevent the sucrose molecules from crystallizing, since agitation or any mechanical disturbance can cause crystallization. By not stirring after the solution boils, disturbances are kept to a minimum.

You can have some more great slimy fun with sugar by exploring what happens to it at different temperatures. Add 360 mL (1½ cups) of sugar to 175 mL of water in a pan and stir thoroughly to dissolve. Heat slowly on the stove and place a candy thermometer in the mixture. When the temperature of each stage in the chart below is reached, remove a spoonful of the sugar solution and place it in a glass of cold water. Then remove it with your fingers and note its properties. You can taste it too, if you wish. It is fascinating to observe all of the different changes that sugar can go through. Different types of candies are produced by heating sugar solutions to different temperatures.

Interestingly, the caramel slime you made reached only the firm ball stage, not the caramel stage. The caramel stage does not taste good at all! If sugar is heated to above the caramel stage, it burns, decomposing into carbon and water vapor. The chart below sums up the changes that sugar undergoes at different temperatures.

Stage	Temp. °C (°F)	Water content	Type of product
Thread	110–113 (230–236)	15%	syrup
Soft ball	113–116 (235–240)	14%	fudge
Firm ball	119–121 (246–250)	13%	caramels
Hard ball	121–129 (250–265)	12%	marshmallows, nougat
Soft crack	132–143 (270–290)	10%	taffy
Hard crack	149–154 (300–310)	2%	butterscotch, peanut brittle
Caramel	160–177 (320–348)	Near 0%	————

Fun fact: A wooden spoon is always used for candy making, because wood is a poor conductor of heat. If a metal spoon is used, it draws heat away from the mixture, potentially causing premature crystallization.

Incredible Edible Slime
Experiment Ten
GLUTEN SLIME!

Gluten is the protein formed when water is added to flour. It is responsible for making dough moldable and elastic. Without gluten, baked goods would never rise in the oven, because gluten helps to hold in the gases formed during baking. Gluten is also a delightfully slimy substance that is fun to mold and stretch.

What you need
- Flour
- Measuring cups
- Bowls
- Oven

Safety precautions
Adult supervision required. Exercise caution when using oven. Do not touch or taste bread until it has cooled.

How to make it
1. Add 240 mL (1 cup) of flour to a bowl.
2. Gradually add 120 mL (½ cup) of water to the dough and work it into the flour until it has a uniform doughy consistency. You may need to use a little less or a little more water.
3. Remove the dough from the bowl and knead it on the countertop for several minutes. If it is really sticky, add a little more flour. It also helps to put some flour on your hands. Knead until the dough

becomes elastic. Do not knead for too long, or the dough will lose its elasticity.

4. Allow the dough to stand for 10 minutes.

5. Place a little of the dough in your mouth and chew on it for several minutes. Note its texture and taste.

6. Place the dough in a bowl of cold water and knead it in the water in order to remove the starch. The water will become cloudy.

7. Empty the water and knead the dough again. Pour off the water and repeat the kneading of the dough underwater. Repeat this process until the water becomes clear. You may need to replace the water 20 or 30 times until it becomes clear. The volume of the dough will be considerably reduced. You are now left with mostly gluten.

What to do with it

1. Note the properties of the gluten. Is it moldable? Is it stretchable? Can you bounce it?

2. Place a piece in your mouth and chew it. Note its taste and texture.

3. Place the dough on a cookie sheet and place in the oven. Heat at about 175°C (350°F) for about 10 to 15 minutes. Cooking times will vary depending on the amount of dough. Keep your eye on it so it does not burn. It should be a golden brown color when done.

4. Use a potholder to remove the bread from the oven. After it has cooled, taste it. What do you notice? Pull the bread apart and observe its structure.

5. Repeat the above experiment using different types of flour. Read the label to check for the amount

of protein (which turns into gluten) in the flour. Use types of flour with differing amounts of protein. Try whole wheat flour, bread flour, cake and pastry flour, instant flour, and gluten flour.

The science behind the slime

When water is added to flour gluten is formed. Gluten forms when two of the proteins found in flour—glutenin and gliaden—react with water. Gluten gives bread dough its body, making it both moldable (plastic) and stretchable (elastic). It provides the supporting framework within bread—like a skeleton. The elastic properties of gluten were once familiar to children raised on wheat farms, who would chew kernels of wheat as a substitute for chewing gum.

Gluten is a protein. Proteins are natural polymers, composed of long chains of amino acid molecules. In gluten, these long chains are coiled and folded together in a large mass. They are very effective at trapping water molecules and forming a gel.

Kneading the bread allows the water to be uniformly mixed throughout the dough. Continued kneading causes these chains of molecules to unfold and arrange in a more regular pattern. As chains of gluten molecules begin to line up, crosslinking occurs between adjacent chains. This causes the dough to become thick and viscous—just like other types of slime you have made.

Without gluten, baked goods could not rise effectively, because the gluten holds in carbon dioxide gas that is released during baking. Just like the rubber of a balloon stretches as it fills with air, gluten stretches when it fills with gas. The bread you made in the above experiment would be considered unleavened bread, since it was made without yeast and thus did not rise. Yeast is a fungus that converts sugar into ethyl alcohol and carbon dioxide (CO_2) gas. It is the CO_2 that causes bread to rise.

The bread you made in this experiment could also be considered low-carbohydrate bread, since most of the starch has been removed. Soaking the dough in water removes the starch, but the gluten is insoluble in water. Gluten molecules do absorb about twice their weight in water, however. The result is a rubbery mass of gluten molecules that are moldable and elastic.

At around 71°C (160°F), the gluten coagulates. Coagulation occurs when the chains of gluten molecules continue to unfold and then bond together. The dough changes from a liquid to a solid. Some water is also lost as the gluten is heated. The bread formed will have a rubbery texture, but will still have a distinctly pleasant taste.

Fun fact: People once believed that the dead body of a drowning victim could be located by placing a bit of mercury in a loaf of bread and setting it afloat. Supposedly, the loaf of bread would float directly over the dead body. This superstition is mentioned in Mark Twain's *Huckleberry Finn*. When Huck Finn finds a loaf of bread that was sent out to locate his presumably dead body, he removes the mercury and eats the bread.

REFERENCES

Becker, Robert. "Ghost Crystals." *Chem Fax*. Flinn Scientific, Inc.: Batavia, Ill., 1996.

Borgford, Christie L. and Summerlin, Lee R. *Chemical Activities*. American Chemical Society: Washington, D.C., 1988.

Branzei, Sylvia. *Grossology: The Science of Really Gross Things*. Addison-Wesley Publishing Company: Reading, MA, 1996.

Cote, Gregory. "Polysaccharides." *Chem Matters*: April 1986; pp. 12-14.

de Zea Bermudez, V. ; Passos de Almeida, P.; and Seita, J. Feria. "How To Learn and Have Fun with Polyvinyl Alcohol." *Journal of Chemical Education*: November 1998: pp. 1410-1418.

Dirr, Michael A. *Manual of Woody Landscape Plants: Fourth Edition*. Stipes Publishing Company: Champaign, Illinois, 1990.

Feldman, David. *A World of Imponderables: The Answers to Life's Most Mystifying Questions*. Galahad Books: New York, 2000.

Gardiner, Anne. *The Inquisitive Cook*. Henry Holt and Company, Inc.: New York, 1998.

Green, Joey. *Polish Your Furniture With Panty Hose.* Hyperion: New York, 1995.

Green, Joey. *Paint Your House With Powdered Milk.* Hyperion: New York, 1996.

Green, Joey. *Clean Your Clothes With Cheez Whiz.* Renaissance Books: Los Angeles, 2000.

Haase, David. "Electrorheological Liquids." *The Physics Teacher*: April 1993; p. 218-219.

Jackson, Ellen. *The Book of Slime.* The Millbrook Press: Brookfield, CT, 1997.

Katz, David A. "A Bag of Slime." *Journal of Chemical Education*: October 1994; pp. 891-892.

Katz, David A. "Chemistry in the Toystore." Presented at the Seventh Biennial Conference on Chemical Education. Oklahoma State University, August 1982.

Katz, David A. "Cooking with Chemistry." Presented at Chem Ed '97. University of Minnesota, August 1997.

Kenda, Margaret and Williams, Phyllis S. *Cooking Wizardry for Kids.* Barron's: Hauppauge, NY, 1990.

Lipscomb, Robert. *Polymer Chemistry.* National Science Teachers Association: Arlington, VA, 1995.

Marsella, Gail. "Silly Putty." *Chem Matters*: April 1986; pp. 15-17.

Marsella, Gail. "Bubblegum." *Chem Matters*: October 1994; pp. 10-12.

McGee, Harold. *On Food and Cooking: The Science and Lore of the Kitchen.* Simon & Schuster: New York, 1984.

Sarquis, Mickey and Sarquis, Jerry. *Fun With Chemistry: A Guidebook of K-12 Activities, Vol. 2.* Institute for Chemical Education: Madison, WI, 1993.

Sarquis, Mickey. *Chain Gang–The Chemistry of Polymers.* Terrific Science Press: Middletown, OH, 1995.

Summerlin, Lee R.; Borgford, Christie L.; and Ealy, Julie B. *Chemical Demonstrations: A Sourcebook for Teachers, Vol. 2.* American Chemical Society: Washington, D.C., 1988.

Waldman, Amy Sue; Schechinger, Linda; Govindarajoo, Geeta; Nowick, James, S.; and Pignolet, Louis H. "The Alginate Demonstration: Polymers, Food Science, and Ion Exchange." *Journal of Chemical Education*: November 1998; pp. 1430-1431.

Walker, Jearl. *The Flying Circus of Physics With Answers.* John Wiley and Sons: New York, 1977.

Wood, Claire G. "Dissolving Plastic." *Chem Matters*: October, 1987; pp. 12-15.

Creative Concoctions brochure by Parent Club. Compass Labs, Inc.; Creative Publishing International, Inc.; Wood-Howard Products, Inc.; and FastMark, Inc.: Palo Alto, CA, 2000.

Clear-Jel® brochure. Educational Innovations, Inc.: Norwalk, CT, 2001.

Insta-Sno™ brochure. Steve Spangler Science, Englewood, CO, 2001.

Instant Snow Polymer brochure. Educational Innovations, Inc.: Norwalk, CT, 2003.

INTERNET REFERENCES

4 Common Gum Products from Seaweed
http://www.philseaweed.com/other.htm

Applesauce Cinnamon Dough Recipe
http://craftsforkids.about.com/library/projects/
blaplcny.htm

Bread Clay
http://craftsforkids.about.com/library/projects/
blbredclay.htm

Food Thickeners (Larry Lippman)
http://www.yarchive.net/chem/thickeners.html

Food Product Design: In the Thick of It
http://foodproductdesign.com/archive/1992/0992QA.html

High Tech Slime Slips Up Suspects
http://www.foxnews.com/printer_friendly_story/
0,3566,41715,00.html

How To Make Electroactive Slime
http://chemistry.about.com/cs/howtos/ht/electroslime.htm

More About Liquids: Thick and Thin
http://www.slb.com/seed/en/notes/liqu_gui.htm

National Play-Doh Day
http://ladygatorsplace.com/play-doh.htm

Newtonian and non-Newtonian fluids
http://www.svce.ac.in/~msubbu/FM-WebBook/Unit-I/
NonNewtonian.htm

Oven Flour Clay Recipe
http://craftsforkids.about.com/library/projects/
blovclay1.htm

Pnut Butter Playdough
http://familycrafts.about.com/library/projects/
blpnutclay.htm

Recipe: Gummi Bears and Jelly Candy Recipes
http://www.recipelink.com

Science of Candy: Caramels Recipe
http://www.exploratorium.edu/cooking/candy/recipe-
caramels.html

Science of Candy: Saltwater Taffy Recipe
http://www.exploratorium.edu/cooking/candy/recipe-
taffy.html

Shear Thinning and Thickening
http://www.newton.dep.anl.gov/askasci/gen99/
gen99944.htm

Silicones
http://www.psrc.usm.edu/macrog/silicone.htm

Silly Putty®
http://inventors.about.com/library/inventors/
blsillyputty.htm

Silly Science
http://www.sillyputty.com

The History of Chewing Gum and Bubble Gum
http://inventors.about.com/library/inventors/blgum.htm

The Page that Dripped Slime!
http://www.freeweb.pdq.net/headstring/slime.htm

Thermoplastics
http://www.psrc.usm.edu/macrog/plastic.htm

Two Types of Polymer Slime
http://www.guidezone.skl.com/polymer2.htm

Viscosity Chart
http://research-equipment.com/viscosity%20chart.html

Slime Notes:_____

_____

_____

_____

_____

_____

_____

_____

_____

_____

_____

_____

Slime Notes:_____

_____

_____

_____

_____

_____

_____

_____

_____

_____

_____

_____

Slime Notes:_____

_____

_____

_____

_____

_____

_____

_____

_____

_____

_____

_____

_____

Slime Notes:_____

_____

_____

_____

_____

_____

_____

_____

_____

_____

_____

_____

Slime Notes:_____

_____

_____

_____

_____

_____

_____

_____

_____

_____

_____

_____

Slime Notes:_____

_____

_____

_____

_____

_____

_____

_____

_____

_____

_____

_____

Slime Notes:_____

_____

_____

_____

_____

_____

_____

_____

_____

_____

_____

_____

_____